BLAMING, SHAMING, AND FRAMING THE IMMIGRANT AS OTHER IN U.S.-MEXICO BORDERLANDS CINEMA:

A DISCURSIVE AND PSYCHOLOGICAL ANALYSIS

By

Viktoria Byczkiewicz

First submitted as a dissertation for the Masters in Applied
Linguistics TESOL at California State University
Los Angeles
Awarded 2005

Chapter 1

Introduction

This study is a critical discourse analysis of contemporary anti-immigrant attitudes in the Mexico-U.S. borderlands. Immigration represents one of the most infernal and heavily avoided of current American domestic issues (Alonso-Zaldivar, 2004), spawned by a global trend toward racism and nationalism during the late 20th century. Capitulation to Anglo- Saxon cultural values and acquisition of the English language are widely touted as necessary requisites to U.S. citizenship (Auster, 2004; Chavez, 1997). The assimilation and integration of new and diverse cultures in the U.S. has vacillated from rapid to languorous resistance, while the status quo maintains a reflexive proclivity toward the rejection of all things foreign, favoring a monoculture. Blanket derision of newcomers who have not readily submitted to forced assimilation can be traced back to Benjamin Franklin who, in the mid-18th century, expressed concern that the German language was threatening linguistic unity and English hegemony (Crawford, 2000; Feagin, 1997). Recently, reconnections to their ethnic origins has sparked both celebration and protest invigorated by a sense of empowerment in Latino communities that refuse to tolerate protracted marginalization or further castigation for their Otherness (Blommaert & Verschueren, 1998; Ono & Sloop, 2002; Simón, 1997). Once proverbial, the fleeting myth of the so-called American 'melting pot'[1] has faded to pipe dream status (D'Souza, 2002; Feagin, 1997).

---

[1] 'Scare quotes' are periodically used throughout this work to warn the reader that the terms contained within them are ideologically problematic. 'Scare quotes' are used to dissociate the writer from the expressions, to "make it clear [the expressions] belong to someone else" (Fairclough, 1989, p. 89).

Extremist U.S. nationals, particularly in the borderlands regions, fervently reject the inevitability of shifting demographic patterns as the 21st century unfolds (e.g., Lerner & Stirling, 1991; Spencer, 2001). Positive concepts of multiculturalism or cultural pluralism are objectionable to nativists who aim to shelter what they wish were an immutable, homogeneous American culture (Blommaert & Verschueren, 1998), though in actuality no such homogeneity exists in the modern world (Wodak, 2001). Blame for economic woes is conveniently displaced onto disempowered migrants who seek to better their lot by claiming their share of the American dream, while heavily guarded international borders serve only to multiply the human suffering (Dunn, 2003; Nevins, 2002).

In this study, naturally occurring data were gleaned from selected documentary film texts for a critical discourse analysis (CDA). Broadly, CDA is concerned with the semiotic power of language in producing social events and processes (Fairclough, 2001). As with nonfiction literature, there exists a tendency to attribute veracity to the documentary film genre, as if the actual beliefs, values, or emotions of a given participant-interlocutor had been dutifully represented without manipulation. Film spectators expect pure or empirical truths from the documentary. However, as Ponech (1997) pointed out, a nonfiction film is decreed so solely by its maker. Documentaries may be informative, yet they must be understood more precisely as argumentative, with the goal of furthering the filmmaker's favored worldview (Nichols, 1991). Some 'social problem' fiction films are also equally feasibly true in their renditions of social conditions and are built around the same theoretical tenets as documentaries: They illustrate a problem, then posit a solution (Berg, 1992; Nichols, 1991). However, for the sake of theoretical simplicity, fiction films were ultimately excluded from this study.

Worldwide, whether or not complete cultural assimilation is possible or even desirable is a sore point and the 'problem' of cultural diversity remains contentiously debated (Blommaert & Verschueren, 1998). From these debates emerges an us-versus-them dialectic, a dynamic that necessitates the Other's existence so as to clearly define another's boundaries. Though peripheral to the main goals of this study, such identity politics are relevant to shaping the hostile attitudes that surface in the anti-immigrant discourse examined here.

This study constitutes a transdisciplinary[2] approach to illuminating an issue addressed chiefly from the view of an applied linguist, drawing on literature from discursive and social psychology, cultural and Chicano studies, Buddhist psychology, and discourse theory.

In Chapter 2, the discipline of discursive psychology, a short discussion on documentary film as evidence for discursive psychological investigation, and recent thought in social psychology on discriminatory attitudes against immigrants are introduced. Lee, Ottati, and Hussain's (2001) fourfold hypothetical construct citing ingroup-outgroup tension, prejudice, national economic concern, and advocacy of obedience to law, together with Short and Magaña's (2002) analysis of political rhetoric, is used to delineate the chief rationales motivating anti-immigrant talk into three categories: nativism, national economic concern, and legal issues. Grassroots actions fueled by these justifications are then briefly described. These include nativism both as a foregrounding attitudinal disposition and a form of political activism, viewed in historical and contemporary contexts (Perea, 1997). California's 1994 Proposition 187 is exemplary of elitist-driven legislation that sought to penalize undocumented immigrants and their children by barring their access to social healthcare and education services (Ono & Sloop, 2002). Official English or English Only movements represent additional efforts to discourage support for diversity and

---

[2] In describing Critical Discourse Analysis (CDA) as a method for social scientific research, Fairclough (2001) distinguished the term transdisciplinary from interdisciplinary. The former more accurately describes CDA in that its "co-engagement" with other social theories and methods "on particular aspects of the social process may give rise to developments of theory and method which shift the boundaries between different theories and methods" (pp. 121-122), potentially internalizing the theoretical logics of the various methods and changing the relationships between them.

immigration in the borderlands (Crawford, 2000). At the federal level, the various 'Operations' of the U.S. Border Patrol have militarized border zones and reinforced justifications relying on the law (Nevins, 2002). Chapter 2 further outlines psychological and linguistic frameworks for understanding blaming, shaming, and Othering, all of which are tactical mechanisms serving to create and reify distance and difference in discourse. Finally, a brief sketch of outlaw or counter-discourse is provided.

Chapter 3 describes the methods and procedures followed in the transcription and analysis of ten film texts, as informed by the literature discussed in Chapter 2 on discursive psychology and Glaser and Strauss's grounded theory (1967), as updated in applications by Wetherell and Potter (1992) and Henwood and Pidgeon (2003) as philosophical approaches to a methodology for analyzing the data.

Chapter 4 presents an analysis of the findings structured in accordance with (1) the categorical codes, axial, and co-axial codes found to correspond to the forces driving various discursive acts (and defined as a result of sorting the data via the grounded theory/discursive psychological approach); and (2) the three chief rationales justifying the anti-immigrant expression.

Chapter 5 concludes the analysis with a discussion of the broader ontological situation of the data and the phenomena in which the data are embedded. It is acknowledged that the issues addressed in the discourse under scrutiny reflect an ideological impasse which reifies a right-wing versus left-wing polarity, thus underscoring the dilemmatic nature of the problem (see Billig, Condor, Edwards, Gane, Middleton, & Radley, 1988). A Buddhist view of the intertwined phenomena of blaming, shaming, and Othering illuminates the underlying psychological processes as attachment to difference (Dockett & North-Schulte, 2003; Nhât Hanh; 2003) and sees the nature of human experience as both socially and subjectively constructed (Bakhtin, 1981; Edwards, 2003; de Silva, 1979; Olendzki, 2003). Finally, Chapter 5 discuses pedagogical implications of the work, examines some of its limitations, and recommends further research.

Statement of the Problem

The perceived threat of Others' encroaching on the territory of anti-immigrant borderlands activists elicits objections so vehement, so rancorous, that protestors' attitudes, as manifest in overt discursive acts, are easily diagnosed as xenophobic. Borderlands tales the world round echo similar sentiments of nationalism, racism, and nativism (Wodak, 2001; see also the *Journal of Borderlands Studies*). However, migration, immigration, and relocation is normative human behavior (Blommaert & Verschueren, 1998). In modern, prosperous nations with exponentially growing populations such as the U.S., the bundle of challenges presented by immigration, including notions of territorialism and cultural supremacy, pose an irresolvable ethical dilemma (Billig, 2001). The social and political conditions that provoke expression of explicitly negative attitudes toward immigrants and immigration are manifold and complex. Generally, in an atmosphere of a large and sustained immigrant influx these conditions include economic insecurity, nativism or territoriality, fear of or sense of being threatened by the unknown other and, ultimately, ignorance (Feagin, 1997; Muller, 1997). For example, since new immigrants have historically been willing to work for less than the rate of pay average among native workers, immigrants are blamed for conniving to 'steal' jobs from Americans (Feagin, 1997; Galán, 1994). Yet as Wodak (2001) opines, "[s]imple conspiracy theories do not seem valid in global societies" (p. 64). Evidence points to the root of this and other problems related to immigration or enculturation as grand-scale forces operating beyond the immediate which erode the quality of life and prevent intercultural symbiosis at local levels. Survival – a relative term – is the impetus for those who are willing to provide 'cheap' labor as well as those who profit from it. Although American labor is available, businesses opt to illegally employ immigrant labor in order to fatten their profit margins (Feagin, 1997; Nevins; 2002; Riker, 1999). This constitutes a vicious cycle wherein the least powerful are blamed for the corrupt actions of those who hold power. Immigrants are blamed for a gamut of social ills – crime, disease, and usurping state welfare benefits. Such public perceptions that immigrants threaten dominant American culture have led to the formation in the Mexico-U.S. borderlands regions of grassroots anti- immigrant groups who rely on scathing, fear-based rhetoric in an effort to keep immigrants out (Perea, 1997).

Purpose of the Study

The aim of this paper is less to explore problematic issues in depth or to map a general psychology of the development of anti-immigrant attitudes than it is to carefully unpack and take stock of the kind of language that is publicly deployed to build a viable body of discourse. Fairclough's (1999) notion of intertextuality and Bakhtin's (1981) dialogic conception of discourse provide useful macro-perspectives. In this view disparate fragments of argumentative talk and discrete filmic texts alike can be understood to build upon and reinforce one another to create a whole body of discourse, or "an internally consistent body of representations" (Riggins, 1997, p. 2) which "[represent] a given social practice from a particular point of view" (Fairclough, 1995, p. 56, as cited in Riggins, 1997, p.2). That is, talk constitutes social practice. The specific purpose of this study is to examine this discursive social practice in the form of candid expression of anti-immigrant attitudes within a corpus of naturally occurring discourse as recorded in situ by independent documentarians in the non-experimental field.

An ancillary pursuit of this inquiry is to explore the language of empowered migrant voices (and those of their advocates) who counter the anti-immigrant discourse, generating what Ono and Sloop (2002) refer to as "outlaw" discourse or, as the name implies, that which falls outside traditionally normative, or sober, bounds. One such exemplary outlaw voice belongs to borderlands artist Guillermo Gómez-Peña, whose subversive performance piece *Border Brujo* (1991) represents an ironic meditation on immigrant stereotypes.

Research Questions

Based on the review of pertinent literature and films, and on the categories which emerged to be most salient in the course of successive readings of the film transcripts (methodology is discussed in Chapter 3), I pose the following research questions with sub- hypotheses:

(1) How is **blaming** the immigrant expressed, explicitly and implicitly, among interlocutors who favor or are opposed to the restriction of immigration and immigrant's rights with regard to:
   (a) economic problems?
   (b) disease and disorder?
   (c) crime?

(2) What role does **shaming** play in framing the borderlands immigrant as inferior with respect to:
   (a) law breaking?
   (b) values and difference?
   (c) language status as a non-native English speaker?

(3) What functions does **Othering** the borderlands immigrant serve:
   (a) in creating an us-versus-them dialectic?
   (b) in rhetoric favoring militarization of the border?

(4) What **counter-discursive** strategies manifest alongside the extreme or mainstream debates on borderlands issues:
   (a) in the form of defense of the migrant worker?
   (b) in the form of protest?

Definition of Terms

Border

The 'border' is regarded equally a socially constructed boundary and a near-two- thousand-mile geophysical barrier, dividing not only friendly nation states but areas with essentially diverse social and cultural characteristics and values. The geographic border was formed in 1848 after the Mexican-U.S. War, but the current conception of the border arose in 1924 when, following the Mexican Revolution, the U.S. government identified the need to protect itself from unwanted Mexican/Latino entrants, leading to the formation of the U.S. Border Patrol (Rodríguez, 1997), for which the government "recruited ex-gunslingers and frontier lawmen" (Ruiz, 1975).

Borderlands

The term 'borderlands' refers to a vaster expanse beyond the geographic border stretching north and south; in the U.S., the borderlands encompass much of California, Arizona, New Mexico, Colorado, and Texas (Anzaldúa, 1999; Fox, 1999). The borderlands also occupy a "psychic space characterized by mixture" (Calvo, 2002, p. 73) which represents a synthetic "contact zone" (Fox, 1999, p. 13) in which potentially fearsome, hybridizing activities take place when cultures collide and mingle (Velasco, 2002). Anzaldúa (1999) referred to borderlands as "a vague and undetermined place created by the emotional residue of an unnatural boundary" (p. 25) (such as that of the nation-state).

Borderlands cinema

The term 'borderlands cinema' encompasses both fiction and documentary films. Borderlands cinema deals with issues of individual, social and cultural anxiety associated with border crossings and collisions, both physical and psychic, and frequently the ambivalence that arises vis-à-vis the Other (Calvo, 2002; Sayles, 1996; Welles, 1958).

Nativism

Nativism is "a term of inherently negative appraisal" (Bosniak, 1997, p. 283) which indicates an ethnic and national bias against perceived foreigners or immigrants. Nativism can denote "strong attachment to a reference group to which one has, so to speak, 'been born'" (Bosniak, 1997, p. 281), leading to the exclusion and derision of others who are perceived to be outside the hegemonic cultural majority.

Blaming

Blaming is defined as the active attribution of causality for an event or condition to a specific or finite cause (Lamb, 1997), very often, a person or group identified as the Other (Dockett & North-Schulte, 2003; Nhât Hanh, 2003).

Shaming
Shaming is meant to convey the psychological sense of oppression which is aroused by repeated or momentary exposure to condescension, humiliation, or intimidation, or by being made the object of social stigma (Falk, 2001; Smith, Webster, Parrott, & Eyre, 2002).

Othering
The term Othering refers to the discursive practice of socially and psychologically differentiating and distancing oneself, or the social group with which one identifies, from an individual and/or his or her social or cultural group.

Discursive Psychology
Discursive psychology, which emerged as an academic discipline in the early 1990s, approaches the qualitative analysis of mind-world relationships strictly via talk, wherein the worldview an interlocutor conveys represents her "common-sense *basis for talking*" (Edwards, 2003, p. 31). Potter (2003) described discursive psychology as "a reworking of . . . what psychology is" (p. 74). It is an interpretive approach to language as performance as carried out by actors in social contexts wherein semiotic interaction is deemed to be a primary manifestation of social practice and the production of social relationships (Fairclough, 2001).

Implications and Limitations
This study has implications for promoting further insight into the discursive and psychological categories by which diverse sectors of the U.S. public (e.g., elites, politicians, or the layperson) view and express arguments on immigration issues, from the standpoint that they perceive themselves to be directly impacted or 'threatened.' I would hope that, if solutions, compromises, or acceptance of cultural Others is ever to be found, this work will illumine the futility of extremism, underscoring the necessity of eliminating abusive, unnecessarily confrontational, or debasing elements from the discourse and alternately infusing the discussion with humaneness, sincerity, tolerance, and a willingness to comprehend. Somewhat paradoxically, this work points up both the intrinsic complexity and utter simplicity of the social problems engendered by intercultural and international contact.

This study is certainly limited in its scope in that all discourse samples were taken from extant film excerpts pre-selected by the films' editors. It is acknowledged that the editing and shaping of the films were conscious constructions in support of the filmmakers' arguments. Outtakes could reveal additionally enlightening data. In addition, the responses of other analysts might yield alternate interpretations. Such is the ambiguous and infinite nature of language. Discourse is understood as constructed, as are the texts ultimately produced by social researchers (van den Berg, Wetherell, & Houtkoop-Steenstra, 2003).

Significance of the Study

The significance of this study lies in its elucidation of the impact of rhetoric which serves to blame and polarize the stereotyped immigrant in public opinion and worldview as part of the ceaseless debate over tolerance for immigration and how to cope with diversity in the modern nation-state (Blommaert & Verschueren, 1998; Wodak, 2001). The nation-state concept is an indispensable backdrop to formulating a collective identity, shaping public opinion, and justifying the denial of racism among anti-immigrant voices (Perea, 1997). The issues and problems dealt with in this thesis have been thoroughly addressed in vast bodies of literature by numerous scholars of immigration studies in every discipline within the social sciences in far greater depth than I am permitted to delve here, or could ever have devoted ample time to address given the limitations imposed on this work of relatively minor scope. What is novel about this study, however, is my focus on anti-immigrant attitudes through a discursive psychological lens with a view to how these attitudes interact with the individual mind and shaping of worldview to provide sufficient motivation to actively participate in blaming and shaming the immigrant.

There are two additional unique features of this work. For one, I augment a traditional Western psychological approach to blame with a Buddhist psychological perspective, which emphasizes a humanistic, practical, and holistic explanation of how the individual mind/persona situates him- or herself in the world (de Silva, 1979; Olendzki, 2003). Second, I sample language used to construct rhetorical argumentation from a corpus of ten select documentary films which, though relatively obscure, remain in public circulation in venues such as academic libraries or public television channels.

Finally, this work is significant in its insistence that blaming, shaming, and Othering are futile endeavors which serve more to deepen the chasms and repeatedly redraft the boundaries between human beings who happen to have been born in different nation-states or speak different languages. As Blommaert and Verschueren (1998) wrote, "people have roots only at the most metaphorical level . . . the need to move around is part of the *condition humaine*. . . Diversity is as inevitable and as restrictive as gravity. It is not to be deplored, nor to be exalted. It is simply there . . ." (p. 14).

Chapter 2

Review of the Literature

The Discursive Psychological Approach

Discursive psychology emerged as a hybrid discipline in the early 1990s, combining research in social psychology, rhetorical strategies, and discourse analysis. Discursive psychology aims to shed light on a broad range of psychological phenomena by analyzing social interaction in fine detail. Of core concern is the critical analysis of attitudes toward issues of racism, sexism, or extremist ideologies as expressed in naturally occurring conversation, particularly in institutional or ideologically charged contexts. Discursive psychology is informed by general theoretical principles of discourse analysis which posit that(1) discourse is the primary means of human interaction, thereby discourse constitutes social action, and these actions are embedded in broader practices; (2) oral discourse is 'situated' in three senses: institutionally, rhetorically, and sequentially (or temporally); and (3) such 'situatedness' informs the ongoing practice of discourse to serve the social and interpersonal interests of interlocutors (Potter, 2003). That is, discursive practice is social interaction that actively both constitutes and reproduces social reality (Fairclough, 1989; Wetherell & Potter, 1992).

Though discourse analysis in general has taken various directions from its post- structuralist origins, a foremost concern remains how talk and texts are carried out performatively by actors in social contexts to effect what in traditional linguistics is referred to as illocutionary force, meaning the force or effect that a speech act has when it is uttered (cf., Austin, 1999; Matthews, 1997). From this orientation, theorists critical of cultural practices have used critical discourse analysis as a tool to unravel epistemologies involving power, competing truths or versions of worldview (Bruner, 1985; Goodman, 1978), Foucault's 'regimes of truth' as represented by so-called expert discourse (Cameron,

Frazer, Harvey, Rampton, & Richardson, 1999) or, in Nichols's (1991) terms, the 'discourses of sobriety' (Fairclough, 2001; van Dijk, 2001).

Potter (2003) holds that "...attitude expressions can be studied as talk designed for use in settings where there is a possibility of argument and where [an interlocutor is] simultaneously justifying a position and implicitly countering alternatives" (p. 74). Psychological activities which typically manifest as talk include "justification, rationalization, categorization, attribution, making sense, naming, blaming and identifying" (Wetherell & Potter, 1992, p. 2). In linking the force of these discursive acts with "collective forms of social action," or the manufacture of ideologies, social analysis is integrated with psychology. "The way descriptions are made to appear factual" (Potter, 2003, p. 73) by drawing upon various discursive or rhetorical resources to construct reality is essential to analyzing the arguments propagated by social actors in confronting others who may be opposed in their values, ideologies, and opinions on how the social system should function. Rhetoric and its reproduction and dispersion as ideology must be examined from the standpoint of its situation within a larger 'conversational' context; every rhetorical utterance is in response to or directed at an interlocutor or projected audience of potential interlocutors.

The great Russian linguist Bakhtin in the 1930s was the first to practically examine language as action (Billig, 2001). Bakhtin recognized that every utterance was situated within a stream of social dynamics and that even the minutiae of communicative language could be interpreted as performance within greater social, historical, and ideological contexts. He claimed that every utterance is dialogic in that it constitutes a response to a previous, assumed, or anticipated utterance (Bakhtin, 1981). A 'true' approximation of meaning can only be inferred in relation to these other utterances, some of which may exist as part of a greater collective conscience, social psyche or historically sanctioned belief system (in Foucaultian terms, truth is "simply an error hardened into unalterable form in the long process of history" (Hartstock,

1990, p. 32)), all of which constitutes an overarching dialogic scheme. Social interaction forms the basis of an individual's psychological state, or mind, including one's attitudes, relative to worldview (Edwards, 2003). Therefore, the study of psychological states in discursive psychological analysis should proceed from the scrutiny of social interaction as manifest in discrete, though inescapably socially situated, utterances. Only through the study of verbal interaction or outwardly projected utterances can attitudes toward social phenomena be elucidated.

Central features of rhetorical, argumentative discourse are criticism of opposition and justification of attitudes, often as position statements in matters of public controversy such as immigration issues (Billig, 2001). According to a classic study, people do not hold attitudes toward mundane matters that evoke little or no sentiment, or toward which there has historically been little public debate or doubt (MacGuire, 1964, as cited in Billig, 2001). The study determined that cultural truisms or beliefs (such as, for example, in Western society, that one should clean one's teeth or bathe) differ qualitatively from attitudes in that attitudes are open to challenge and mutually treated as issues up for debate. One's position on whether unauthorized immigrants should be stringently deterred from entry or granted the same human rights as U.S. citizens can be characterized as an attitude rather than a belief. Once an issue has been challenged, it is subject to the proffering of further opinion which exposes a variety of attitudes. In expressing attitudes, interlocutors make reference to notions that they consider to be commonsense but which in fact reveal ideological assumptions and expectations about themselves, society, and the world (Billig, 2001; Edwards, 2003; Fairclough, 1989). Ideological discourse becomes popular discourse, is recognized as 'truth,' and begins to operate as acceptable, effective rhetoric (Wetherell & Potter, 1992, p. 61). As Bakhtin (1981) observed, each unique utterance is tied to an ideological history which ingrains ways of thinking and behaving so that ideas seem 'natural' or unquestionable to a given society's members. It is through dominant ideology that social inequities are made to appear as natural or inevitable (Billig, 2001), as well as how unequal power relations are sustained (Fairclough, 1989). Attitudinal expressions represent social actions performed by way of words, as illustrated by the example of prejudice and discrimination across groups. Prejudice is expressed via "the verbal repetition of stereotypes, while discrimination involves behavior, or the putting of prejudiced words into practice. However, if acts of discrimination are examined in detail, one can see that the distinction between words and actions soon collapses" (Billig, 2001, pp. 215-216).

Analysis in discursive psychology focuses on "performance in the form of video and audio-recorded and transcribed records of interaction" (Potter, 2003, p. 73) and extends to a wide array of texts documenting a host of interactive contexts in institutional, clinical, and communicative settings, all venues in which meanings are negotiated and normative social practices are performed, challenged, and reified. Research is purely qualitative in that it is not concerned with 'the influence of X on Y' but rather with 'how X is done' (Potter, 2003; Ratcliff, 2003). This kind of microanalysis necessitates the in-depth exploration of processes description and repetition – rather than merely outcomes. The analytical procedures adopted by the discursive psychological approach are quite similar to those provided by Glaser and Strauss's (1967) grounded theory paradigm in generating data and deriving analytical questions and categories directly from textual sources rather than via working from preconceived hypotheses. This theoretical framework for analysis has provided a foundation for practitioners of discursive psychology who study social psychological interaction with a view to identifying ideological themes and markers as "instantiated in ordinary talk," as opposed to exposing the attitudinal system of individual speakers. Utterances are located as part of broader social processes of replicating and reproducing discursive themes and ideologies, and maintaining social discursive practices (Billig, 2001; Fairclough, 1989; van Dijk, 1991; Wetherell & Potter, 1992).

Documentary Film as Evidence for Discursive Psychological Investigation

The precise aims of this study are to examine the expression of negative stereotypical attitudes towards immigrants as represented in select documentary or social problem films, and to point up how these attitudes function to blame, shame, and frame immigrants as Others. These aims are in line with those characteristic of a discursive psychological study that analyzes potentially controversial talk in which interlocutors are impelled to justify and defend their own arguments while fending off those of others (Potter, 2003). Films that feature interlocutors arguing over immigration issues in the borderlands provide superb evidence for discursive psychological investigation.

It would be a mistake to assume that the director of a documentary had less control over actors than those in fiction films – the documentary director merely exercises the appearance of non-intervention by representing actors who present convincingly naturalistic performances of themselves. The documentary or social problem film constructs an idiosyncratic reality by shaping a case for the way the world is using its own internal logic, vying with others' logics to lend legitimacy to a favored version of reality (Nichols, 1991). Documentary and fiction films alike represent their preferred iteration of reality; each is equipped to pursue identical points. A fiction film might be distinguishable from a nonfiction film owing only to the filmmaker's designation (Ponech, 1997). However, documentary functions explicitly to advance an argument, particular perspective, or sensibility, whereas the social problem narrative does so implicitly (Nichols, 1991). In the documentary a problem is outlined and solutions are proposed, sometimes ostensibly by social actors, but ordinarily by the filmmaker, either tacitly or forthright. The blurring of the demarcation between traditionally separate genres was eloquently discussed by Geertz (1980) at the onslaught of the 'crisis of representation' which marked a paradigmatic revolution in the social sciences a quarter century ago (cf., Kuhn, 1962/1996).

It must be emphasized that documentary film is itself a mode or social research and reporting, particularly in its interactive mode when "textual authority shifts toward the social actors recruited" whose "comments and responses provide a central part of the film's argument" (Nichols, 1991, p. 44). In the interactive documentary mode, the dynamic between the filmmaker and actors creates a synergy that actively engages the viewer in an unfolding social drama. Actors are momentarily vested with ample floor time to explain themselves. Still, the filmmaker retains rhetorical control, as does the discourse analyst or social researcher vis-à-vis his or her subjects, by posing specific questions or reporting or editing to match a preferred flow of logic – which may also be someone else's explication of reality. In Nichols's (1991) critique, "interviews are a form of hierarchical discourse deriving from the unequal distribution of power" (p. 47), an observation extensively investigated in a collection of papers edited by van den Berg, Wetherell, and Houtkoop-Steenstra (2003) which scrutinize the use of the interview as a research instrument "very often taken for granted" (p. 3) as a means of making reliable inferences in the social sciences. An analogy between the interactive documentary format and the discursive psychologist's interview format is reasonable in that both assume the methodical gathering of information to build a verifiable base of knowledge (see also Cameron et al., 1999). This creates the appearance that the social researcher is an authority on matters under investigation, when in fact s/he is constructing yet another textual interpretation of reality (Fairclough, 1989).

Attitudes towards Immigrants and Immigration A Social Psychological Model

Fundamental social and cultural values are responsible for determining people's beliefs and attitudes toward others (Dockett & North-Schulte, 2003). Lee and Ottati (2002) and Lee, Ottati, and Hussain (2001) proposed four hypotheses to explain social and political discrimination against Mexicans. The two affective hypotheses are (1) the *ethnic ingroup favoritism hypothesis* and (2) the *prejudice and racism hypothesis*. The two cognitive hypotheses are (3) the *national economic concern hypothesis* and (4) the *obedience to law hypothesis.*

As implied, the *ethnic ingroup favoritism hypothesis* projects that members of a given socially dominant group, or 'insiders,' will tend to view themselves more favorably than they do 'outsiders.' Strong identification or affiliation with a group by default engenders favoritism; however, since prejudice is a visceral reaction, deeply culturally entrenched sociocultural beliefs and practices serve as preservation instincts. Prejudice and racism, however, can develop independent of the personal inclination to bolster or favor the interests of one's group; a prejudiced individual may not necessarily identify with any ingroup.

In the *prejudice and racism hypothesis,* Lee et al. (2001) observed that "[p]rejudice toward people of Hispanic descent may be rooted in gut-level affective reactions derived from childhood socialization, the belief that Hispanics undermine cherished American values (e.g., the work ethic), or both" (p. 432). Prejudice against outsiders can also be read as the assignment of stigma, or the marking and devaluation of the other as flawed "and somehow less than fully human" (Dovidio, Major, & Crocker, 2000, p. 3). Falk (2001) describes stigmatization as insiders' means of drawing an invisible barrier around outsiders in order to deny admission to their inner circle. Regardless of actual behavior, deviance is forever imputed to the stigmatized outsider, whose plight serves as a cautionary tale to potential immigrants who would deign to trespass ingroup boundaries or resist pressure to conform to American social norms.

The *national economic concern hypothesis* stems from anxiety that the economic security of the United States is being undermined by immigration (Lee et al., 2001). Muller (1997) noted that anti-immigrant sentiment peaks during economically unstable periods when unemployment and job loss are high and earnings stagnant. Such state of affairs conveniently fuels the targeting of the immigrant as culpable, in spite of being an overly simplistic, misdirected, and even paranoid response (Feagin, 1997). "Liberals" are also blamed

(Spencer, 2001). Mexican migrant workers rebut that the Anglo majority is unwilling to perform the strenuous manual labor or 'dirty work' that they gladly accept (Akers, 2004; Courtney, 2001; Espinosa, 1989; Ruiz, 1975). Johnson (1997) characterizes Americans as "schizophrenic in [their] views about undocumented Mexican labor" because while Mexicans are accurately perceived to be hardworking and willing to perform tasks that many Americans find unsavory and are glad to delegate, at the same time they "serve as scapegoats when the U.S. economy turns for the worse" (p. 171). This kind of ambivalence (Calvo, 2002) is symptomatic of the dilemmatic nature of the immigration 'problem' (Billig et al., 1988; Billig, 2001). In actuality, large corporations and small businesses alike are eager for cheap labor to enhance their profit margins (Akers, 2004; Feagin, 1997; Marin & MacGregor, 1998; Riker, 1999).

Finally, Lee and Ottati (2002) and Lee et al. (2001) proposed the *obedience to law hypothesis*. Obedience to the strictures imposed by the legal system is highly valued by U.S. citizens who unwaveringly "perceive any illegal activity as a threat to social order" (p. 621 & p. 433) and summarily criminalize those who violate what some consider arbitrary legal limits. Often this stance is taken by vigilantes whose xenophobia is so intense that they would rather witness border crossers die of thirst than give them water to drink (Annerino, 1999; Nevins, 2002). The various military interventions or 'Operations' implemented by the U.S. Border Patrol have functioned to lend credibility to the law, yet their most important impact may have been to appease anti-immigrant factions (Galán, 1994). Still, Muller (1997) argues that "it is not as much the legal status of aliens but rather their ethnic, cultural, and religious diversity that is the origin of most anti-immigrant sentiment" (p. 115).

Over a five-year period of mounting anti-immigrant sentiment in the mid-1990s Short and Magaña (2002) analyzed newspaper accounts of political candidates' rhetorical characterizations of Mexican immigration and identified three main themes which corroborate Lee et al.'s (2001) model: (a) issues of legality, (b) economic implications, and (c) issues of nativism. In this framework, nativism supplants Lee et al.'s (2001) two affective hypotheses.

Grassroots Expression of Anti-immigrant Sentiment

The following five subsections address ways of looking at anti-immigrant sentiment as grassroots expression. At the broadest level, it is necessary to explore nativism, a concept which actively reemerged in the literature of the mid-1980s to interpret renewed public furor when shifting migration patterns began dramatically changing borderlands demographics (Bosniak, 1997). Second, California's Proposition 187 is briefly examined as a potent contemporary example of legislative action fueled by nativism (Nevins, 2002). Third, Operation Gatekeeper, the first of the U.S. Border Patrol's efforts toward militarization of the international boundary as a strategy for deterring immigrants from crossing, is touched upon. Next, the phenomenon of Mexican-Americans who favor stringent legislative measures concerning immigration issues is covered. Finally, alongside the sentiment that gave rise to Proposition 187 are movements in favor of eliminating bilingual education programs entirely and establishing English as the official language of the U.S. These interrelated phenomena all involve discursive maneuvers of blaming, shaming, and Othering to further condemnation of migrant/immigrant border crossers.

Nativism in the U.S.: Its historical context and contemporary resurgence

Nativism in the individual stems from an irrational fear of the Other (also known as xenophobia), typically in reaction to unfamiliar physical traits or language as well as political hostilities. In the U.S., xenophobia manifested as intense hatred of Germans, German Americans, and the virtual banning of the German language during World War I (Crawford, 2000), and similar sentiment was aimed at the Japanese and Japanese Americans during World War II (Perea, 1997). Nativism is a variation of racism, with the difference that its objects of derision are 'foreigners' instead of native-born minorities or members of underclasses. The language nativists use to justify this automatic exclusion underscores the inherent privilege of birthplace; natal affiliation rather than one's humanity takes precedence (Bosniak, 1997). This matter is complicated in the Mexico-U.S. borderlands by its history of shifting political claims to territory.

Anti-foreigner sentiment peaked in the 1840s, the 1890s, the 1920s and the 1950s, with the latest wave in the 1990s (Nevins, 2002; Perea, 1997). These eras share at least three elements: a rampant sense of economic fragility; a steady and sizeable flow of immigrants; and obvious disparities between the social, cultural, and ethnic makeup of new immigrant arrivals and the majority of the established U.S. population (Muller, 1997). While xenophobia is currently primarily directed toward Latino and Asian immigrants, Mexicans are arguably America's favorite contemporary scapegoat (Short & Magaña, 2002). Events which have ignited the recent resurgence of anti-immigration attitudes include the liberal reform of immigration laws, a continued influx of unauthorized immigrants, and the thawing of the Cold War (Feagin, 1997). The terrorist attacks of September 11, 2001 further exacerbated already heightening nativistic sentiment and legitimated the need for enhanced border security (Perea, 1997).

Nativist activism in the borderlands takes negative social attitudes towards immigrants to an extreme level as demonstrated by public rallies decrying immigrant rights, often in the name of the law (Espinosa, 1989; Kelly, 2005a & 2005b; Lerner & Stirling, 1991). Pet nativist pursuits entail restricting entry, policing international borders, and promoting legislative efforts to curtail immigrant inflow. Of great historical import is the Immigration Act of 1924, which established a national origins quota system mandating immigration proportional to the ethnic composition of the U.S. population of 1890, thus giving preference to northern Europeans and severely limiting immigration from Africa and Asia. The measure was in part a backlash against surges of immigrants from southern and eastern Europe. (Incidentally, the U.S. Border Patrol was established in the same year.) National origins quotas were abolished by 1965 Amendments to the Immigration and Nationality Act which had been supported by President John F. Kennedy (Borjas, 2004), but not without vociferous opposition by such nationalist groups as the Daughters of the American Revolution, who argued that relaxing immigration policy would lead to an increase in "mental health and retardation problems" and unduly burden the already "heavy laden taxpayer" (Duncan, 2004, p. 65). The most recent examples of legislation inspired by nativist-spawned activism are California's Proposition 187 (Nevins, 2002; Ono & Sloop, 2002) and Arizona's Proposition 200 (Marosi, 2004).

Nativism intensifies as immigrants are perceived to threaten blue collar jobs during economically challenging times. The act of blaming the immigrant for stealing American jobs, in addition to problems such as crime, disease, and the degradation of the 'American' lifestyle, epitomizes the nature of nativist dogma, which is premised on the conviction that the economy would improve by restricting immigration (Lee & Ottati, 2002). Feagin (1997) and (Borjas, 2004) identify more powerful global economic forces as determining national economic conditions, especially capitalists' decisions to invest in labor abroad and domestic employers' preference for cheap sources of labor resulting in reductions in well-paying domestic job opportunities.

Less pronounced within mainstream anti-immigrant discourse, though at the heart of nativist sentiment, are blatantly racist and exclusionary appeals (Wetherell & Potter, 1992), as exemplified by 1992 and 1996 presidential candidate Patrick Buchanan's position that immigration should be abolished altogether (Feagin, 1997). Buchanan blames what he perceives to be the deterioration of American demographic and cultural ideals on "the cultural left that hates America and wants to destroy it [and] no doubt ... see[s] mass immigration from Third World countries as a handy way of achieving that" (Auster, 2004, p. 73). Mexicans, likely because they have constituted the greatest percentage of immigrants in recent decades (de la Garza & DeSipio, 1998), in particular pique Buchanan's ire. Non- native, technically legitimate residents who maintain ties to their countries of origin are also targeted because, it is argued, they consume social resources more appropriately allocated to native-born Americans (Galán, 1994). This point is disputed by immigrants and their advocates as "intense opposition to an internal minority on the ground of its foreign (i.e., 'un-American') connections" (Higham, 1988, as cited in Bosniak, p. 281). Billig (2001) refers to the established state of affairs in affluent nations as 'banal' nationalism; that is, the privileges enjoyed by legal citizens residing within the boundaries of the nation-state are regarded as normative and taken for granted:

"In the modern age, the notion of national identity has been bound up with the notion of the nation-state. Today, these notions appear commonplace and solid, so that it is difficult to imagine that in previous ages communities were not imagined in this way. The assumptions of nationhood have seeped through contemporary consciousness, so that the nation-state appears as a 'natural' form of community." (Billig, 1995 as cited in Billig, 2001, p. 219)

The nation-state imposes the necessity of a boundary, in part inuring the psychological imperative of a boundary, among other less tangible ones, in the minds of abiding citizens.

Legislative measures: California's Proposition 187
California's Proposition 187, which passed on November 8, 1994, represents the most successful attempt at legally codifying anti-immigrant sentiment to date. Its premise was to ameliorate fiscal problems, but the underlying intent was to discourage unauthorized Mexican immigrants from entering the U.S. by denying them the provision of public healthcare, education, and other social benefits (Bosniak, 1997). Having saturated the newspaper and television media, the rhetoric used to achieve its passage represents "some of the most virulent racist discourse in the history of the U.S." (Ono & Sloop, 2002, p. 3). As numerous articles in the *Los Angeles*

Times suggested, the notion that good upstanding citizens should exhibit strict observance of the law in large part underscored the rationale buttressing Proposition 187 (Ono & Sloop, 2002; Santa Ana, 2002). Only emergency medical care would be conceded (Lee & Ottati, 2002). The proposition threatened to oust non-native English speaking schoolchildren from the state's educational institutions, a punitive move instilling fear and panic among both parents and children, as poignantly captured by Laura Angelica Simón in the acclaimed documentary film, *Fear and Learning at Hoover Elementary* (1997).

Clearly, the proposition primarily targeted Mexicans (Michelson, 2001). Then- governor Pete Wilson, one of its chief supporters, based his successful re-election campaign on the premise that the state's support of Mexican 'illegals' robbed California natives of their rightful bounty in a state beleaguered by debt (Magaña, 2003). In further blaming all immigrants for the state budget crisis, "Wilson undoubtedly set the stage for immigrant bashing" (Nevins, 2002, p. 85). The discourse surrounding Proposition 187 had an indelible impact on popular perceptions and gave license to the liberal expression of anti-immigrant sentiment that had already surfaced following the Immigration Reform and Control Act (IRCA) of 1986, which offered amnesty to undocumented immigrants already residing in the U.S. Ono and Sloop (2002) argue that due to its ubiquity in the mainstream media, the pro-Proposition 187 discourse fundamentally influenced publicly acknowledged concepts of "nation" and "border," enticing the public away from the romantic idea of the U.S. as a haven for immigrants. Newspaper and television items encouraged embracing the proposition as a means of protecting California and the U.S. from becoming a "Third World" country, framing Mexican immigrants a threat to "the cohesiveness of the country's culture" (Nevins, 2002, p. 114). These media profoundly contributed to the shaping of political opinion by characterizing Mexicans both "legal" and "illegal" as "bad" and "immoral," and culpable for environmental problems and overpopulation (Nevins, 2002). Immigrants were shown as diseased, unhygienic animals, posing a public health threat to "us" and "our children" (Santa Ana, 2002). Such negative representations reinforced and legitimated existing anti-immigrant sentiment and irrevocably altered race relations.

"[W]hen racial categories become intertwined with political initiatives," wrote Short and Magaña (2002), "favoring or opposing the political initiatives themselves can become opportunities for people to discriminate against particular populations without being socially reprimanded and accused of bigotry." One can disguise prejudicial attitudes "by championing political initiatives that appeal to universal abstract principles such as justice, egalitarianism, and equity" (p. 702), or by moral appeal to the necessity of enforcing the law (Lee & Ottati, 2002). Van Dijk (1997) concurs, calling talk falsely premised on humanitarian values "elite racism" (p. 31); Wetherell and Potter (1992) discuss how contemporary politicians have become adept at masking prejudice in conducting racist discourse by conveniently eliminating the race category, and Riggins (1997) calls this conscious deletion as an attempt to "mitigate and disguise" (p. 7). A strategy of moral high- grounding diverts the issue of racism (or ethnicism, the modern equivalent to racism in which "culture substitutes for race" (van Dijk, 1997, p. 33)) to one of *obedience to law*. Having broken the law permits insiders to portray negatively constructed outsiders with dehumanizing stereotypes in constitutionally sanctioned free speech venues. Rigid adherence to legal principles holds that if a Mexican immigrant has entered the U.S. illegally, that person has technically engaged in criminal behavior. The 'criminal' label psychologically facilitates discrimination against other members of that same ethnic group regardless of their national origin (Short & Magaña, 2002).

There has historically existed an ambivalence about the presence of Mexican workers in California. The *bracero* program, essentially a guest-worker arrangement which lasted from 1943 to 1965, invited much-needed agricultural expertise. Through this program Mexican workers provided the main thrust to an economic boon which turned California into an agricultural giant. The *bracero* program helped establish positive impressions of Mexican workers in California, and such images were evoked in opposition to Proposition 187. While these favorable images were intended to conjure sympathy for underpaid laborers whose work strengthened the economy but went largely unappreciated, proponents reinforced the idea that undocumented Mexicans were largely welfare recipients who leeched precious state monies (Nevins, 2002). Further, even if they did work hard, they were still depicted as dirty and uncivilized (Nevins, 2002; Santa Ana, 2002). In this spirit, Pete Wilson advocated a guest-worker program (much like that initially proposed by President George W. Bush during his 2004 re-election campaign) which could realistically be likened to the temporary exploitation of workers' bargain labor (Magaña, 2003). However, the rhetoric of Proposition 187 reduced undocumented immigrants to mere human capital. The centrality of cost concerns in bolstering the legitimacy of arguments about immigrants, particularly whether as "economic units" they strengthen or drain the economy, remains widely acceptable among both proponents and opponents of the measure as evinced by repeated explicit arguments over their contribution to the nation (Bosniak, 1997; Ono & Sloop, 2002, p. 31; Peek, 2001). The admission that Mexican workers are an asset to the economy while precluding their entitlement to social benefits is a recurrent dilemma clouding arguments about immigrant labor. Praise and blame simultaneously function to enforce a racial hierarchy which permanently objectifies and marginalizes the Other in a shroud of ambivalence.

The use of deictic pronominal categories labels "them," the illegitimate outsiders, as insidious to "us," presumed insiders whose cultural purity is threatened by "their" penetration (Carbó, 1997). Additional divisive terminology brands unauthorized immigrants as 'criminal' for having disregarded the law by "taking cuts" before those who patiently await their visas by observing legal procedural channels. One *Los Angeles Times* piece characterized illegal border crossers as people whose lives as "would-be American[s]" begin as criminals (Laguna, 1994, as cited in Ono & Sloop, p. 58). As claimed

Pat Buchanan, in such cases punishment is in order, lest "the message ... go out to a desperate world: America is wide open. All you need to do is get there and get in" (Buchanan, 1994, as cited in Ono & Sloop, 2002, p. 60).

Another slant pitted the state of California against the federal government, creating yet another divisive "us" and "them" polarity. Then-Governor Pete Wilson and his supporters nurtured this "local-nativist versus outsider-nationalist division" (Ono & Sloop, 2002, p. 61) with reference to the metaphor of the subservient state asserting its right to seal and monitor its borders in a manner deemed appropriate by its local inhabitants after suffering the consequences of a lax federal authority (Ono & Sloop, 2002). Wilson's mostly Republican camp also proposed amending the law so that children born in the U.S. to undocumented immigrants could no longer automatically become citizens (Nevins, 2002).[3]

There are many reasons why people vote for or against certain initiatives, and certainly racial attitude is not the sole factor, nor is political affiliation. Short and Magaña (2002) claim that the upsurge in anti-immigration rhetoric, "relative political apathy" (p. 703) among Mexican American citizens, and generally poor impressions of the INS (now a division of the U.S. Department of Homeland Security) have lent credence to politicians' popular project to scapegoat Mexicans and swayed prejudicial attitudes. Such political rhetoric

---

[3] In Arizona, similar legislation, Proposition 200, which requires proof of immigration status in exchange for social benefits (including some as mundane as library cards) passed on November 2, 2004 (Marosi, 2004). Arizona has seen the closure or near-closure of borderlands medical facilities due to Mexicans using them without being able to pay for services rendered. Residents have complained that the Border Patrol will not pick up illegal immigrants because the federal government would then be required to reimburse hospitals for the care provided. (Kelly, 2004).

embellishes and stimulates further discourse which perpetuates, distributes, and normalizes negative representations of Mexicans, encouraging nationalism and nativism.

The U.S. Border Patrol's Operation Gatekeeper

An anti-immigrant line of reasoning might presume that, as relegated to object status, immigrants must be 'contained' by the border, as "they" are likely to exploit valuable resources which should rightly go to "us." With the passage of the North American Free Trade Agreement (NAFTA) in 1994, the free flow of international exchange and increasing economic integration led the U.S. federal government to determine that a once-porous border ought to be more tightly controlled by the U.S. Border Patrol, since additional cross-border traffic encouraged human smuggling (Muller, 1997). This Clinton-administration- sanctioned move was officially termed Operation Gatekeeper, and targeted the San Diego/Tijuana sister cities area, the most heavily trafficked U.S.-Mexico border crossing.[4] Although Operation Gatekeeper enhanced militarization of the border to discourage the free movement of human beings, over the six-year period (1994 to 2000) following NAFTA's initiation trade inflows and outflows increased by 250%. A "borderless economy and a barricaded border" (Nevins, 2002, p. 169) seems paradoxical. From a global perspective, the international boundary between the U.S. and Mexico has become increasingly irrelevant as trade has increased manifold, yet Operation Gatekeeper has encumbered what were once routine crossings by unauthorized immigrants. Unauthorized passages have been diverted to the arid deserts of Arizona and New Mexico (mostly the former), which has incurred a dramatic rise in deaths from dehydration and exhaustion (Annerino, 1999; Nevins, 2002; Peek, 2001).

---

[4] In 2002, nearly 300,000 Mexican workers legally crossed the border on a daily or weekly basis in order to work in the United States (Nevins, 2002, p. 5).

Given that "state boundaries are an extremely powerful symbol of national identity and sovereignty" (Nevins, 2002, p. 161), Nevins views Operation Gatekeeper as a nation- state-building project, one covert purpose of which was to emphasize the illegality of unauthorized entrants' actions and further castigate, shame, and criminalize Mexican immigrants in the American public psyche. The militarily fortified boundary, argues Nevins, deepened the territorial chasm between "us" and "them" and further polarized social positionings. At the same time, Operation Gatekeeper ensured that the well-to-do could continue to profit by exploiting the influx of cheap labor which, should it cease to be illegal, would also cease to be cheap labor (Davis, in his foreword to Nevins, 2002, p. x). The "war on illegals" was one consequence of a marked recession in the economy of Southern California in the early 1990s that spurred several violent incidents, vigilantism (Lerner & Stirling, 1991; Peek, 2001), and 'restrictionist' grassroots activism (among groups such as *Light Up the Border*), especially in the San Diego area, where border crossings were at the time highest. Ultimately, Operation Gatekeeper "helped create a climate that . . . condoned this violence towards undocumented immigrants" (Palafox, as cited in Peek, 2001).

Mexican-Americans in favor of stringent legislative measures

It is not unusual for immigrant Latinos or Mexican Americans to identify and align themselves with the larger ingroup or Anglo majority in favoring increasingly restrictive immigration policy (de la Garza & DeSipio, 1998). Some immigrants incline toward conservatism in their newly adopted country. The desire to fit and assimilate, to find acceptance and security, and to go relatively unnoticed as an Other by the 'natives' necessitates conformity (D'Souza, 2002; Magaña, 2003; Shaver, 1985).

The Mexican American majority in El Paso, Texas demonstrated strong support for the U.S. Border Patrol's heavy-handed Operation Blockade/Hold-the-Line project, much like their predominantly Euro-American counterparts in the sister border city of San Diego. Nevins (2002) explains this seemingly contradictory phenomenon from the perspective of identity politics, admonishing that the proximity of Mexico to the U.S. does not dictate that Mexican Americans, the sizeable population living in the borderlands included, are any less 'American' than those of other ethnic origins or more distant nations. Latino and Mexican Americans generally oppose restrictive immigration and border-control measures in greater proportion than the general population because of such policies' blatant discrimination against people of Mexican descent; however, as individuals, identity-based allegiances do not necessarily lie primarily with ethnic heritage: "[W]hile many [Mexican Americans] often strongly distinguish themselves from non-Mexican Americans and embrace their Mexican heritage, [some] also often harbor strong anti-Mexican sentiment" (Nevins, 2002, p. 83). Binder, Polinard, and Wrinkle (1997) explain this in reporting that "because of their cultural affinity with nations south of the U.S. border" (p. 325) Latinos generally oppose highly restrictive immigration measures; however, ethnicity is not the primary factor motivating these attitudes. Rather, "the more integrated the Latino populations are into American society" (p. 326), the more their attitudes toward immigrants will come to resemble those of the dominant majority. In addition, de la Garza and DeSipio (1998) found that non-citizen Mexican-Americans were generally opposed to current levels of immigration, perhaps in part because of the labor competition new immigrants represent. During the 1950s, many Mexican American organizations opposed the *bracero* program and did not object to deportations of immigrant workers "in an effort to distance themselves from immigrants" (Gutiérrez, 1995, as cited in Michelson, 2001, p. 60). However, *Tejanos* (i.e., Texan Mexican Americans) advocated more stringent barrier controls than Latinos in California.

The Official English movement

Anti-immigrant activists frequently cite immigrants' limited English ability as problematic (Tatalovich, 1997). Strong accents, learner interlanguage, or low ability peeves nativists who perceive lack of fluency as a threat to the social welfare system and to national unity. Nativists reason that immigrants cannot obtain gainful employment if their English skills are sub-par, and advocate the total abandonment of native language use as a means of assimilating into the mainstream. In particular, 'Hispanophobia' evinces anxiety about a changing cultural and linguistic landscape, and the ascendancy of anti-immigrant organizations from the 1980s has lent greater impetus to the Official English movement (Crawford, 2000), which regularly introduces to Congress a constitutional amendment to make English the national official language (Feagin, 1997).

The U.S. government has never explicitly defined an official language policy, although individual states, predominantly the more homogeneous states in the south, have passed laws in favor of Official English, mostly during the 1980s and 1990s (Feagin, 1997; Porter, 1996).[5]

Prior to this uprising period of nativist backlash, only three states had official English laws. Established in the 1983 by Senator S. I. Hayakawa (a Japanese immigrant) of California, the most prominent group favoring instituting national policy remains U.S. English. Its Web site claims that "the passage of English as the official language will help to expand opportunities for immigrants to learn and speak English, the single greatest empowering tool that immigrants must have to succeed" (retrieved on 4 February 2005 from the Web site http://www.us-english.org). Crawford (2000), however, contends that the organization's concern is only ostensibly about language. Its covert agenda aims to stunt increasing diversity and multiculturalism: "By seizing on language as a symbol of what troubled them about immigrants, Anglo-Americans could register a protest without seeming bigoted"

---

[5] As of this writing, the total number of states having Official English laws is 27.

to the public eye (p. 32). Anti-Hispanic, anti-Catholic sentiment factors into the equation. The Catholic religion's rejection of birth control, leading to stereotypes of Latin hypersexuality (Nevins, 2002), and Latinos' presumed disregard for the environment, are too overtly racist assessments to be publicly voiced.

English-only advocates' fear of diversity and fear of the Other have led to the protest of foreign languages seeming to permanently weave their way into the social landscape. They object to business or street signs in Spanish or Chinese, which to them signify public acceptance of linguistic and cultural diversity. Outraged nativists' calls for the restriction of foreign language use actually constitute "a demand to reinforce the existing social order," i.e., the dominance of Anglo-Saxon cultural and linguistic norms and values (Crawford, 2000, p. 27).

Proponents of Official English policies routinely resort to the argument that American English is being threatened with extinction by Spanish, suggesting that contemporary immigrants refuse to learn English. They erroneously compare today's immigrants to yesteryear's European immigrants, claiming that whereas earlier European immigrants willingly acquired English, today's immigrants refuse to do so. Studies by Alba (2004), de la Garza and DeSipio (1998), and Veltman (1983, 1988, as cited by Crawford, 2000, p. 6) directly debunk this myth; in fact, Mexicans and other native-Spanish-speaking immigrants from Latin America are just as if not more eager to acquire English as a Second Language as immigrants have ever been and, with the exception of those inhabiting relatively isolated areas, Anglicization is now occurring more rapidly everywhere. Previously, immigrant families had lost their native languages by the third generation; today, this is happening already by the second generation. Furthermore, in stark contrast to earlier immigrants, only a minute fraction of newcomers from the 1980s onward have spoken no English, since moderate-to-extensive English language education in schools has become standard worldwide. Surveys have consistently shown that most Mexican Americans are bilingual and that immigrant parents completely accept the importance of their children learning English in school (Feagin, 1997); they have also received greater exposure to Anglo-American culture through the media. It may only seem on the surface as if Mexican immigrants are not acquiring English because, representing the highest proportion of immigrants to the U.S., Mexicans continue to arrive steadily and thus maintain high visibility (de la Garza & DeSipio, 1998). In fact, de la Garza and De Sipio (1998) found that Mexican Americans who had not obtained U.S. citizenship held strong convictions that people residing in the U.S. should learn English. By the same token, American social institutions, in particular educational establishments, are so deeply invested in capitalist America that schools quickly train children "to fit in and accept the existing system of class relations" (Fairclough, 1989, p. 33). Schools are breeding grounds where children learn their place in the social hierarchy and are given the tools they need to survive given their rank (Ollman, 2002). This is certainly the case with respect to language and ethnicity. Ultimately, today's immigrants are savvier than those of a century ago, fully aware of the power that knowledge of English bestows to them, and of its utility as a hot commodity (Fairclough, 1989).

The Discursive Construction of the Other

Language is central to constructing the Other. It is within the domain of social interaction that the marginalization, devaluation, dehumanization, and silencing of minorities by majority social groups is effected. Wherever power, privilege, or human social hierarchies exist, authoritative texts, from political speeches to academic treatises to mainstream media, function to manipulate public perceptions. Ideologues, who orchestrate the language that achieves these manipulations, are notorious for attempting to instill "ideological uniformity" (Fairclough, 1989, p. 86), a form of intellectual subjugation. To prevent the division of a people, they aim to craft the image of "a single enemy" (p. 86) and project a unified sense of national identity. Garnering a unified front against a singular, unambiguous threat is easier than responding in kind to a diffusion of nondescript Others.

Fairclough's (1999) notion of intertextuality provides an interesting theoretical frame here. Intertextuality refers to how texts interact among and reinforce one another to create a complete body of discourse or "internally consistent body of representations" (Riggins, 1997, p. 2) which "represents a given social practice from a particular point of view" (Fairclough, 1995, as cited in Riggins, 1997, p. 2). By means of intertextual reinforcement, the social practices of stereotyping and constructing bias facilitate the legitimation of blaming and shaming the Other for social ills. Blaming and shaming rhetoric ultimately distends discord and maintains an imbalance of power among ethnic and national groups.

This rhetoric of Othering and exclusivity facilitates exploitation in political and economic spheres and contributes to the reproduction of ideological power (Fairclough, 1989; Riggins, 1997). Simplistic, stereotyping rhetoric is readily reproduced by people who may have little or no experience or knowledge of a subject yet nevertheless trust in the authority of texts and thus formulate and express opinions based on accessible ideologies. Such intertextual processes of social interaction and reproduction construct the social realities that reverberate as true or common sense (Falk, 2001). In this manner, much of the anti- immigrant vitriol – sanitized and implicit or explicit – circulates within the public domain. In their analyses of discourse on racial diversity, Blommaert and Verschueren (1998) identified talk about Others using four basic categories: implicit negative, implicit positive, explicit negative, and explicit positive.

Some attention to the word Other itself is also in order. In this study, the Other constitutes a deictic category. The *Oxford Concise Dictionary of Linguistics* (1997) defines deixis as "the way in which the reference of certain elements in a sentence is determined in relation to a specific speaker and addressee and a specific time and place of utterance" (p. 89). In other words, the verbal construction of the Other is relative to the context in which the reference is uttered. Other can refer to almost anything or anyone; it is an 'empty' variable. Psychological attribution theory explains the defining of the Other by its attachment to an identifiable attribute, such as blameworthiness (Shaver, 1985). The Other is elusive, exotic, compelling, and both attractive and repulsive. In its repulsiveness, the Other becomes untouchable, a contaminant. People are impelled to locate this deictic Other in order to recognize what they are not. As Sartre (1965) put it, "I need the Other in order to realize fully all the structures of my being" (as cited in Riggins, 1997, p. 5). Hartstock (1990) later pointed out that "the Other is always seen as a Not, as a lack, a void, as deficient in the valued qualities of society" (p. 22). The Other belongs to a "chaotic, disorganized, and anonymous collectivity" (p. 22) and cannot shed the stigma of his or her group affiliation nor be appraised individually, as separate from the group. S/he is a dehumanized object who functions to meet the needs of the more powerful, by tending to their gardens, children, and domestic chores.

These framings of the Other reflect the idea that linguistic interaction is at base fundamental human action which corresponds to Bakhtin's dialogic principle that "all human relations, including that to oneself, are mediated by language and the other..." (Stam, 1989, p. 5). The notion that oral discourse is situated within meaningful, historical context and that this situation contributes to its continued construction relates to Bakhtin's (1981) notion that all utterances are in direct reaction to a previous utterance. Every word "presupposes an interlocutor" (Stam, 1989, p. 11) because human beings exist only for and through the Other.

Othering is the byproduct of social identity formation which entails classifying people into different categories, aligning the self with an ingroup, and in comparing that ingroup to other groups formulating the conclusion that one's own group is superior to others. In the philosophy of Mahayana Buddhism, this process of forming one's social identity "encourages attachment to difference," which is the underlying cause of inter-ethnic tensions (Dockett & North-Schulte, 2003, p. 220).

The public condemnation or expression of disapproval or

intolerance of the Other is today more complex because tolerance of diversity has become at least prescriptively normative in most contexts in the U.S. (Blommaert & Verschueren, 1998; Riggins, 1997). Euphemisms, the armature of the politically correct, have reached new heights of sophistication. The term *immigrant* has etched out that of *foreigner* with its inerasable connotation of Otherness. Lexical terms are used to mitigate and disguise prejudice, to modify and soften opinions (Fairclough, 1989), though no form of representation can be taken at face value; we must not confuse the "represented world of the text with the world outside the text" (Stam, 1989, p. 11).

Pronouns are inherently inclusive or exclusive: we ⇔ they; us ⇔ them; ours ⇔ theirs. Add to this: Self ⇔ Other. When speakers talk about Others, they contribute to those Others' social identities, naming and defining them within a reproducible sphere of social interaction. Prejudicial or deictic discourse disguises elite racist or ethnicist objectives by manipulating the pronominal system to convey messages of inclusion when the intent is actually otherwise. Carbó (1997) uncovered the use of this linguistic ploy in her study of Mexican political debates from which she determined that the syntactic component of discourse carries "decisive elements of the ideological force of discursive events" (p. 92). A 1990 public address made by then-President Carlos Salinas revealed contradictions between the implications of the words and syntax. His clever choice of the pronouns 'our' and 'we' to imply ingroup or outgroup status elucidated inherent ideological contradictions and facilitated avoiding any overt acknowledgment of indigenous Indian peoples' Otherness in relation to Mexico's ruling elites. In illuminating the subtle rhetorical force of grammatical forms, Carbó offers a meta-perspective on how discourses about the Other can reveal even more about the observer or the speaker than the Other being observed. Such analyses show that masterful rhetorical play can succeed in making a persuasive case without being overly argumentative (Nichols, 1991). The stereotyping of Others is achieved by repetitive inculcation into the social conscience in order to maintain the appropriate distance between 'us' and 'them.'

The Discursive Practice of Blaming

Attribution theory, a focal area within social psychology, suggests that immutable cultural values affect the 'naïve' or 'ordinary' perceiver's "judgments of causality, responsibility, and culpability" (Shaver, 1985, p. 2), and that the assignment of blame for events or situations, consciously or not, may be strongly influenced by personal motives. Blaming to salvage one's own lot, or self-serving bias, is the common stuff of scapegoating (Dockett & North-Schulte, 2003; Guimond, Begin & Palmer, 1989). The cognitive process of assigning blame begins with an epistemic search for a sequence of events for which someone must be held accountable, though it may be that there is no particularly blameworthy referent; explanation lies in a complex congruence of multiple circumstances and events. Shaver (1985) explains that the psychologist's "attributional analysis of blame assumes that an effect will be seen as the consequence not of one single antecedent, but as the consequence of a subset of the possible conditions" (p. 32). In alignment with a Buddhist psychological model, attribution theory acknowledges the convergence of multiple conditions, some observable, some hidden, as cause for any given social phenomenon.

Blaming entails judgment, and situational or circumstantial factors are bound to present complications to incur error in making judgments (Shaver, 1985). Just as demarcating an outgroup has been likened to drawing an invisible boundary around stigmatized Others (Falk, 2001) or forming one's sense of social identity involves classifying others who seem different, the cognitive process of attribution entails identifying "invariant properties of people and features of the social environment" (Shaver, 1985, p. 6). This may be delusional, however, being that social landscapes are permanently in flux (Nhât Hanh, 2003). Further, as Guimond, Begin, and Palmer (1989) suggested, educational background and professional socialization play an undeniably important role in whether individuals adhere to a 'person-blaming' ideology or a 'system-blaming' ideology. A social sciences

38

education predisposes one to find fault for difficulties competing in a capitalistic economy with the system rather than with the individual, whereas individuals trained in business tend to locate blame with the individual for his economic hardship.

It is necessary to differentiate between how people assign blame for events and how they explain others' actions. Whereas the antecedents to events may include causes other than human actions, it may be "reasonable to argue that true personal causality for action might be limited to intentional behavior" (Shaver, 1985, p. 38). Causation must involve *human agency*, which is considered to be the "central feature of causality within an attributional theory of blame" (Shaver, 1985, p. 32). For behavior to qualify as blameworthy, it should involve volitional action. Observable human actions, too, may involve prior causes, which paints an increasingly complicated picture. In applying this model to the issues addressed in this work, it becomes clear that blaming the immigrant/Other is highly reductionistic activity and undermines the complex interplay of factors responsible for social and political conditions. Blaming the Other can also indicate a sense of entitlement to humanitarian privileges that that Other cannot claim (Lamb, 1996). For example, in committing an act of abuse or violence, anger fueling the perpetrator leads him to justify blaming the vulnerable target/Other. In foisting blame onto an innocent, or attributing blameworthy or shameful qualities to another, a person reveals her "foolish" bias. A vast literature attests to people's "tendency to externalize blame for bad outcomes" (Tennen & Affleck, 1990, p. 216), even when bluntly committed by their own hand. Making excuses is a popular variation on adapting to new or exacting circumstances, with blaming another person the quintessential excuse by shifting the focus entirely away from the self.

The Vietnamese Zen Buddhist monk Thich Nhât Hanh describes a perpetual pattern of suffering and strife behind the social interactions among Others at odds:

"Suffering, unhappiness, violence, and war escalate when we

are overcome with anger and try to punish and inflict suffering on the other side. We act this way because we believe that as a result we will suffer less, but of course this action only leads to the other side desiring revenge. This is the surest course of destruction. ... When we suffer, we blame the other person or group. We hope that if we can punish them and make them suffer, we will feel better and gain some relief. We know the disastrous effects of such behavior, yet we continue to follow this course. The result is more unhappiness, more terrorism, more violence, and more war." (Nhât Hanh, 2003, pp. 91-92)

This push-pull scenario easily applies to the struggle among actors on opposite sides of the Mexico-U.S. immigration imbroglio. From a Buddhist psychological perspective, blaming is partly construed as evidence of the rejection of responsibility for one's own reactions to the unfolding of situations. Often blaming is the only recourse when envisioned outcomes fail to materialize, or life circumstances disappoint. In blaming, one denies responsibility for an undesirable situation and thereby believes he is excused from finding solutions to conflicts. Concern for solutions which bode best for a community or nation seldom has priority over ensuring individual satisfaction. Western clinical psychologists, traditionally, are less concerned with the general wellbeing of the community and helping the individual to achieve integration into that community than they are with helping the individual to attain personal happiness. American citizens may be 'entitled' to the pursuit of personal happiness; however, individual happiness is not always in the best interests of the larger community (Lamb, 1996; Verkuyten, 2003).

Though blaming is viewed to be justifiable in the Buddhist context when an act is clearly committed with intention (de Silva, 1979, p. 73), blaming as institutionalized social practice creates a vicious cycle of displacing anger for the situation at hand onto an undeserving Other, a phenomenon bound to occur when power or clout is uneven or, as Dockett and North-Schulte (2003) explain, when a person is psychologically attached to the recognition of difference in the

Other. To deny responsibility for one's own reactions to another's actions or to blame another for situations to which multiple causal factors are involved is, in Zen Buddhist thought, to defy a fundamental tenet of mature personhood. In attributing personal responsibility for an action to another, one concurrently and oft unwittingly attributes personal force or power to that person as well (Shaver, 1985). "The trouble with blame," states Lamb (1996) plainly, "is this all or nothingness, this black and whiteness" (p. 12). The black-and-white stance of extremism typically questions who is inherently 'good' or 'right' and who is 'bad' or 'wrong,' as if absolute assignments of character were possible. In the Buddhist perspective, all human beings contain the seeds of both good and evil (de Silva, 1979). Lamb chastises the quintessential blamer for his "other- directed stance." It "seems hypocritical," she admonishes, "to be advocating a self-reflective stance for others" (p. 11) when one can barely come to terms with oneself. To point the finger at all, one must be willing to apportion a share of the blame to oneself. In Buddhist reasoning, finger-pointing triggers a never-ending cycle of having the finger pointed back, then pointing the finger again, ad infinitum. As an internally consistent body, the anti- immigrant discourse displays this characteristic of perpetual reactivity.

Giving in to a discursive cycle of blaming leads to the desire for vengeance (Lamb, 1997), a primary force motivating the collective activities of anti-immigrant groups like Light Up the Border (see Galán, 1994; Lerner & Stirling, 1991), U.S. English, the American Patrol/Voices of Citizens Together (2001), and the independently spurred 'citizens' arrests' of vigilante stalkers like the notorious Barnett brothers of Arizona (Palafox, 2000). Blaming as acceptable social practice casts undocumented immigrants as scapegoats for conditions often beyond their power, the larger realities of the impacts of global political economy obfuscated.

The Discursive Practice of Shaming
The illocutionary force of a discursive act of blaming has the capacity to function further as an act of shaming. Shaming is

41

defined here as a deliberate move to cause "another person to feel shame, usually through some form of public censure or approbation" for violating or opposing mainstream social norms (Smith et al., 2002, p. 157). Akin to humiliation and to the less damaging, usually fleeting, feeling of embarrassment, shame is detrimental to the personality in incurring a lasting sense that there is something inherently wrong about oneself (Brothers, 2005). This could be the deeply humiliating shame associated with the stigma of poverty (hooks, 1994), or the shame which results from having engaged in criminal behavior (though criminality is more aptly associated with guilt). When one believes one has committed a wrongful act, s/he often experiences feelings of regret or remorse (Smith et al., 2002). In either case, these are two kinds of stigma which are alike in that both poverty and having a criminal history are characteristics which, under most circumstances, one attempts to conceal.

Public exposure of alleged deviance or moral transgression prone to negative social judgment has historically been linked to shame, as determined by Smith et al. (2002) in an extensive review of literary material and scientific data. They came to the general conclusion that explicit "public exposure enhances shame regardless of whether a person believes his or her transgression violates a personal standard" (Smith et al., 2002, p. 145). Stigma is the residue of negative stereotyping or labeling via "generalizing from an observable physical attribute to a set of assumed traits" (Biernat & Dovidio, 2000, p. 88), and the unshakeable result of shaming. Among the three types of stigma identified by Goffman (1963), "tribal identity," such as race, religion, or national origin[6] (as cited in Biernat & Dovidio, 2000), is relevant to this inquiry. The process of stigmatizing involves noticing that an individual is

---

[6] Goffman (1963) also named "blemishes of individual character" (e.g., mental illness or addictive behavior); and "abominations of the body" (physical irregularities, such as a birthmark or deformity) as additional stigmatic categories (see Biernat & Dovidio, 2000).

different from the norm or ingroup, and devaluing that person as a consequence (Dovidio, Major, & Crocker, 2000). Viewing a human being in terms of a single differentiating characteristic and for that reason treating him or her adversely is tantamount to calling into question that person's full humanity. This leads to the internalization of the stereotype by the stigmatized and, frequently, shame.

Prevailing social norms enable the stigmatizer to feel justified in maltreating, avoiding, or excluding the stigmatized (Crandall, 2000). A hierarchical social reality is accepted by the majority as truth which justifies the assignment of permanently unequal status to groups, leaving the stigmatized ashamed at occupying a lower rung (Crandall, 2000) or for having an "unwanted identity" exposed (Smith et al., 2002, p. 157). This occurs because, from a conservative or nativistic standpoint, the stigmatized individual is deemed to be responsible for his or her stigma, as reinforced by the subtle blaming, pejorative, or condescending rhetoric propagated by politicians, journalists, academicians, and other arbiters of social truth. Political realities tend to dictate that immigrants will be classified as representatives of the group with which they appear to be affiliated regardless of the extent of their ingroup involvement or personal sense of identification; stigma attaches by association.

Significant research shows that political conservatism correlates with "a tendency to make attributions for outcomes" (Crandall, 2000, p. 136), which supports Guimond et al.'s (1989) hypothesis that capitalistic/business-oriented ideologies favor person-blaming over system-blaming. The Protestant work ethic and the belief that a hierarchical ranking of individuals is a good and natural system of social relations cushion these fundamental lay beliefs. Ideologies justifying hierarchical social relations figure significantly in the formulation of public policy concerning matters of immigration and provide both moral and psychological rationale for according fewer privileges to stigmatized groups. According to Alicke (2000), in making justifications for withholding privileges, one attempts to emphasize the positive aspects of what are otherwise harmful actions.

Shaming by use of pejorative terminology has an impact that reverberates throughout the generations. The use of the term "illegals" to define suspected undocumented immigrants or noncitizens began to circulate in common parlance around 1954, when Operation Wetback, a massive deportation scheme, was implemented. Prior to this time unauthorized immigrants had been referred to as "aliens," "illegitimates," or "ineligible" immigrants. Media shifted to the use of the term "illegal" for it was viewed as the least offensive label (Nevins, 2002). In Otto Santa Ana's view, the label "illegal" represents the imposition of a semantic concept or "text image" onto the Mexican immigrant (personal communication, May 27, 2004) which, as Professor John Ramirez (CSULA) observed, is a label that has aggressively stuck (personal communication, March 10, 2005). Permanent residents are at present officially called "resident aliens."

Counter-Discourse or Outlaw Discourse

Outlaw discourse refers to rhetoric originating in marginalized communities which adheres to logics lying outside the accepted logics of dominant discourse (Ono & Sloop, 2002). It involves nurturing a culture of resistance to dominant discursive representations by crossing borders and inventing new ways of seeing and speaking about experience (hooks, 1991). Outlaw logics are relatively invisible forms of protest; only when introduced to the public arena might they gain visibility in mainstream discourse communities. Outlaw logic challenges the cultural truisms prevalent in mainstream thinking, suggests an alternative worldview, and has the potential to foment social change. In Ono and Sloop's view, "successful outlaw logic must change the way normative judgments are made" (2002, p. 143). For example, the assertion that the New World Order/Border means that there are no more margins, so no more "Others" either, but rather a "utopian cartography" in which "hybridity becomes the dominant culture … and monoculture becomes a culture of resistance practiced by stubborn Caucasian minorities" (Gómez-Peña, 1994, p. 213) exemplifies outlaw logic contending to upset widespread normative thinking (cf. Fox, 1999).

Ono and Sloop (2002) studied postings to an electronic discussion board, which they consider to be an invisible forum for discourse, and found several recurrent themes connected to California's Proposition 187, among them the theme of identity or identification and notions of citizenship. Having a strong sense of identification was found to be unifying at the level of the nation-state but divisive by excluding some membership in the nation-state and as a result inspiring the formulation of external or alternative groups. In the postings, participants called for a redefinition of the nation-state as well as new means of identification which would transcend affiliation at the restrictive level of the nation-state. Eschewing familiar us-and-them ways of thinking, outlaws alternatively propose that people rethink their relationships to one another in terms of spiritual unity (as in "we are all children of God" or "of the universe"), common histories ("we are all immigrants"), or in terms of internationally sanctioned human rights which should morally supersede the legal rights granted by the spurious nation-state entity. Appeals to notions of global citizenry and "a world without borders" (Ono & Sloop, 2002, p. 153) are common in outlaw discourse (see also Bosniak, 1997).

Guerilla theater is a common manifestation in the realm of outlaw discourse. This includes radical performance activism on college campuses, such as when students at the University of Wisconsin at Madison circulated on campus posing as INS agents, demanding to see students' ID cards as proof of their legitimacy. Alternative performance theatrical spaces and media tend to rely on ritual and irony. Guillermo Gómez-Peña's (1991) film *Border Brujo* does so by "interrogat[ing] and expos[ing] the prejudice exercised on the "modern" Other" (Velasco, p. 214), upsetting dominant logics and skillfully subverting the balance of discursive power (Gómez-Peña, 1994).

Majority and minority discourses each exhibit distinctive

features (Riggins, 1997). The discourses produced by dominant majority groups tend to be "univocal" and "monologic," whereas minority discourses are more likely to be "contradictory, complex, and ironic" (p. 6). Humor and satire operate effectively in minority discourse; however, "[i]ntermingled with the celebratory and defiant discourses of the minority Self may be lingering elements of shame and self-hatred, a result of exposure to the dominant culture's educational institutions and to psychological masochism" (Riggins, 1997, p. 7).

A Foreword on Methodological Preference

Cameron et al. (1999) are of the opinion that "interaction [with social actors] enhances our understanding of what we observe, while the claims made for non-interaction as a guarantee of objectivity and validity are philosophically naïve" (p. 155). In other words, when a researcher assesses social 'reality' from a positivistic stance, s/he purports to have an advantage of distanced, objective insight. On the other hand, when a researcher acknowledges her part in creating a text by interacting with social actors she admits to the inescapability of her own subjective cast on the interpretation of data. This acknowledgment of the validity of multiple realities from multiple perspectives is the stance of the qualitative relativist who rejects quantitative reductionism (Gardner, 1983; Geertz, 1984). It is also the stance of the Buddhist thinker aware of construing experience from moment to moment.

Actors' reported experiences, as represented in the films which provide discursive data samples for this study, are either counted as genuine or discarded as spurious. Filmmakers have the power to represent, manipulate, or re-contextualize the opinions given by actors to suit their line of argumentation (Nichols, 1991), and this is borne in mind in assessing the anti-immigrant attitudes expressed. The uniqueness of understandings and intentions also figure directly into the analytical equation; the researcher should, to the extent possible, be wary of ascribing identical intent to identically appearing utterances, or of assuming that respondents mean the same thing just because identical utterances have been made (Cameron et al., 1999).

Chapter 3

Methodology and Research Design

The discursive psychological method applied in this study represents a natural outgrowth of grounded theory as an approach to interpreting transcripts in social scientific research (Billig, 2001; Glaser & Strauss, 1967; Potter, 2003; Wetherell & Potter, 1992). The analytical procedures similar to these paradigms involve generating analytical categories and questions directly from textual sources rather than seeking to validate preconceived hypotheses or establishing questions *a priori*. Data are transcribed, then freely coded, categorized, and re-categorized (Lindlof & Taylor, 2002; Potter, 2003). This approach insists on the use of naturalistic data for purely interpretive, qualitative analysis and rejects the quantification of discourse (Wetherell & Potter, 1992). A grounded theory/discursive psychological approach provides a cohesive, interpretive, and critical accounting of anti-immigrant attitudes as found in 'naturally occurring' nonfictional discursive representations. I chose to tap into previously recorded film texts to explore attitudes toward immigrants vis-à-vis prominent issues relevant to migration or immigration in the U.S.-Mexico borderlands.

Rationale for Methodological Approach
Since documentary and social problem films typically follow an argumentative narrative structure and deal with controversial issues, they represent an appropriate source of material suitable for the social-psychological study of discourse. Life unedited meanders, rendering the task of linguistic data collection by observational or other real time fieldwork methods exacting and time-consuming. The mining of film and video intentionally crafted to address a targeted topic helps the qualitatively oriented researcher to economize (somewhat) on data collection time, eases the burden of handling cumbersome equipment, and eliminates reliance on forced or otherwise spurious data as potentially generated by

quantitative approaches to the study of discourse. I firmly share Potter's (2003) view that it is preferable "to go straight to the setting instead of eliciting talk about the setting" (p. 81) and therefore dismiss the Discourse Completion Task (DCT) as a viable course of inquiry. Social actors play themselves more realistically *in situ*, not when hypothesizing about conjectured actions. This posture celebrates '*anti* anti-relativism' as discussed by Geertz in his seminal 1984 article. Documentaries that depict actors' immediate impulses in real-life anti- immigrant demonstrations are presumed to be more naturalistic and veracious than the type of reflective data that could be culled by questionnaire or survey in an experimental setting.

The accessibility of pertinent films and videos was sufficient reason alone to pursue using film as evidence for analysis. Since discursive psychological analysis requires naturally occurring data and avoids reliance on discrete, unsituated utterances from a sample of recruited participants, establishing personal distance to interlocutors by drawing on extant films already published for public consumption neutralizes tentative ethical considerations in targeting human subjects specifically for conducting social research (Cameron et al., 1999). That the language represented consists of a filmmaker's patchwork is unproblematic: Drawing on film samples that are an editorial product parallels linguists' common practice of extracting data samples from corpora of print media, such as newspaper articles. Arguably, print media resides a generation even further removed from 'reality,' mediated to a greater degree, than audiovisual media in which an interlocutor's likeness remains visually and vocally intact.

A final rationale for tapping into extant films for data is my previous graduate training in conducting qualitative field research with a video camera as instrument following the philosophies and methods advocated by visual anthropologists including Collier and Collier (1986) and former teachers Richard Chalfen, Jayasinhji Jhala, and Jay Ruby of Temple University. The strong tug of this methodological background justifies a longstanding personal preference for a purely qualitative approach to social scientific study.

The Grounded Theory Approach to Social Scientific Research

In the mid-1960s sociologists William Glaser and Anselm Strauss coined the term 'grounded theory' to justify a rigorously defined qualitative methodology at a time when both social and physical scientists from a broad range of disciplines aggressively advocated quantitative methods, citing their greater reliability (Glaser & Strauss, 1967; Henwood & Pidgeon, 2003). By the late 1980s, qualitative research psychologists came to favor a grounded theory framework, having realized its utility in creatively approaching substantive problems from a principled and practical perspective, especially in attributing qualities to discourse (Henwood & Pidgeon, 2003).

Grounded theory results from generating codes, categories, and further axial and coaxial categories or subsets from psychological phenomena. Through a process of constant comparison of categorical data, a core category, to which all others are related, eventually emerges. From this process of analytical induction evolves or emerges a hypothesis – or research question(s) – alongside ongoing observations (Lindlof & Taylor, 2002). The refinement of possible explanations continues until regularly observed examples lead to the declaration of a hypothetical behavioral "law" (Ratcliff, 2003). The epistemology informing this process is best described as constructivist in nature (Henwood & Pidgeon, 2003).

Understanding social and linguistic research as constructed illuminates the researcher's role as creatively engaged in an ongoing interpretive process of "generating new understandings and theory" (Henwood & Pidgeon, 2003, p. 134) or, new ways of seeing. Grounded theorists maintain awareness of being rooted in their "particular individual, institutional, and other socioculturally embedded perspectives and locations" (Henwood & Pidgeon, 2003, p. 135; cf. van den Berg, Wetherell, & Houtkoop-Steenstra, 2003). This epistemological orientation is reminiscent of Bruner's (1985) actual worlds or Goodman's (1978) symbolic ones, wherein the recognition of multiple and alternate realities is at once legitimate and contestable; there are infinite ways of seeing, hearing, thinking, structuring one's universe of knowledge, and consequently assigning meaning to the multiple, fragmented, and ever-shifting discursive activities that order these frameworks. Such is the nature of discourse; it is social action which reinvents or affirms realities.\

The grounded theory approach to social scientific research may draw upon a wealth of textual sources including interviews, field or case-study notes, taped recordings, and archival or library holdings. Talk is characterized as socially situated process which is logically embedded in a larger discourse. Analysis focuses on the unfolding of discursive processes, not static or decontextualized language, in order to adduce theoretical categories (Charmaz, 2004).

In devising a grounded theory for the study of anti-immigrant attitudes as depicted in selected films, a three-phase process was followed. Phase I involved generating multiple questions and taking note of particularly "intriguing or troubling phenomena" (Charmaz, 2004) during initial film screenings for data discovery. Phase II concentrated on preparing transcripts and generating codes, categories, and axial and co-axial categories. Phase III entailed analyzing the data by making constant comparisons of highlighted transcripted material, then integrating insights and patterns into a theoretically cohesive work.

Phase I: Process of Data Discovery and Selection of Films for Analysis

The first phase of this research entailed the selection of films for analysis by identifying issues around which conflict surfaced as the broadest working category. One distinction of the grounded theory approach is the researcher's early identification of a particular topic which piques her interest. She then follows the thread of inquiry that openly leads through developmental twists and turns, and sometimes dead ends, before landing at an underlying question. My initial determination was to locate extant films available through university facilities which focally addressed issues connected to "illegal" or undocumented immigration within the vicinity of the U.S.-Mexico borderlands, and from these to glean data that portrayed distinct attitudes toward the salient issues explored in the films.

Selecting films for analysis entailed a time- and labor-intensive process of searching for, identifying, and locating films which fit criteria related to the general goals of the study, categorizing films thematically, and finally deciding which would make the final cut for analysis. Texts by Maciel and Racho (2000) and Noriega (2000) partly facilitated the way in this regard. Films were screened based on accessibility. From the start I followed a fuzzily articulated interest in conflicts as arising from differentials in social power and looked exclusively for documentary films potentially containing dialogue as evidence of uneven power dynamics between native and non-native speakers of English (or, U.S. citizens and non-U.S. citizens), as well as grander dialogic schemes between filmmaker-as-interlocutor and audience-as-interlocutor (with Bakhtin's (1981) framework in mind). This launched a circuitous period of discovery during which I screened numerous films that somehow addressed conflict, tension, or skewed dynamics of power. The Mullins Music and Media Center at California State University, Los Angeles houses an ample collection of video artifacts, and the university's Educational Opportunity Program has also amassed a substantive video collection relevant to the ongoing debates over immigration and intergroup relations. Initial searches revealed that issues continuing to arouse great fervor have been significantly enduring and engaging to warrant the copious production of both documentary and fiction films dealing with various sub-topics.

While my broadest initial direction was inequities of power in discourse, gradually it made sense to gravitate toward a geographically focused study, and to hone in on borderlands cinema. By limiting the field and scope of enquiry geographically, cultural conflicts pitting populations against one another by native language and geographic origin were highlighted. Film viewings at this stage also revealed several significant thematic categories relative to borderlands issues including the murder of migrant women laborers and other hate crimes committed against migrants, matters of economic or legal concern, territoriality, and restrictionism, protectionism or nativism. Controlling, regulating, or manipulating human border traffic emerged as a central problem. The problem of nativism, which entails a sense of superiority or greater entitlement to human rights over non-citizens based on geographic, cultural, and linguistic claims to origin, has resurfaced as a central sensibility in political struggles throughout American history, and turned up prominently in the rhetoric of a number of films in service of the social process of justifying and fueling anti- immigrant attitudes.

This first stage of data collection was devoted to free and instinctive note-taking during initial film screenings on factors such as the main issues being showcased, the featured roles of social actors/interlocutors (e.g., immigrant, activist, community member, government representative), any immediate impressions, reactions, suspicions or associations with the content, and messages perceived to be suggestive of the filmmaker's position. My initial goal was to generate multiple questions and to take notice of "intriguing or troubling phenomena" while viewing the films. Of primary import was to ask the fundamental question, "What is happening here?" (Charmaz, 2004), to which the simplest initial answer was that actors were displaying anti-immigrant attitudes in venting their frustrations and anger about a variety of social problems, and that these expressions took discursive shape as blaming, scapegoating, and shaming immigrant others.

Recalling the social psychological theories alluded to in Chapter 2, attitudinal expressions are typically highlighted in controversial dialogic contexts which may call for simultaneously explicitly justifying one's position while implicitly countering alternatives. With this in mind, I sought out films containing representations of critical thematic concern or extremist ideologies having relevance beyond an immediately personal scope to carry wider social implications. When a filmmaker elicits or captures frank opinion-giving on these volatile issues, he positions the social actor within the ontological universe of a film of his own construction or may also allow the actor the leverage to position him- or herself within the scope of the project. Multiple situational factors coincide to incite the actor to engage in opinion-giving or position-declarative speech acts (or, as preferred here, discursive acts). An initial discovery was that explicitly negative remarks and stereotyping were typically indicative of anti-immigrant attitudes. Themes revisited in a number of films dealing with borderlands issues included what could be construed as racist or ethnicist talk, condescension and humiliation, the inhumane framing of the Other, instances of deictically distancing the ingroup from the outgroup, or 'us' from 'them,' advocacy of harsh punishments for lawbreakers, indifference to the fate or well-being of immigrants, and the exploitation of migrant workers for capitalist gain.

About 30 films were considered in total. One lamentable fact made clear during data discovery was the paucity of available films with a distinctively anti-immigrant authorial voice, as the library's holdings reflect typically liberal or left-wing leanings. The Internet proved to be the sole source of obtaining video made from anti-immigrant perspectives. A three-pack from the American Patrol (Voices of Citizens Together) cost $45, and Americans for Immigration Control sold a ten-minute item for $10. Just one of the films from the American Patrol (edited by Glenn Spencer) was included in the final database, since the data in the three-pack were generally redundant. Otherwise, the films screened were made by individuals or entities displaying sympathetic attitudes toward the borderlands immigrant's plight. It was found that filmmakers espousing an *anti* anti-immigrant ideology tended to portray immigration 'restrictionists' in the worst possible light, whereas anti-immigrationists featured in the films also tended to portray their opposition at their most extreme.

In addition, the selection of film excerpts for analysis was almost entirely restricted to anti-immigrant sentiments originally expressed in English, following Fairclough's (1999) sentiment that relying on translated data should be avoided in the event of inaccurate representation. Translations in films represent interpretations of the Spanish-language voices. Some subtitled texts, among them instances of counter-discourse, were included in transcripts as an attempt to accurately contextualize the English-language utterances under scrutiny. As my Spanish-language proficiency is rudimentary, it was necessary to rely – to a limited extent – on translated subtitles to facilitate situating cross-utterances. In doing so, translations provided by filmmakers were trusted to be relatively reliable or reasonably representative of the original Spanish-language utterance.

Phase II: Generating Categories and Codes and Transcription

Following the initial period of screening and brainstorming, in Phase II it was necessary to create transcriptions and to evaluate the texts for amenability to more precise research aims which became clearer as the data discovery process progressed. At this point a first wave of films from among those screened was eliminated from consideration for analysis. Following Wetherell and Potter (1992), the method of transcription was a minimized version of the Jeffersonian system which "included speech errors, pauses and gross changes of volume and emphasis, but ignored most features to do with speed, breathing and intonation" (p. 100). Narration was also transcribed and added to the data bank, in representation of the text's author. (See Appendix A for transcription conventions.)

In some cases, especially with the shorter documentary pieces, I transcribed entire films. However, in the case of other films "focused transcription" (Ratcliff, 2003, p. 117), was determined to be sufficient. This is because some films contained data that was definitely mostly irrelevant to the study at hand, such as extensive biographical information about the actors, or expository scripted commentary by an off-camera narrator. In addition, since I chose to focus on data provided in the original English language, some (but not all, so as to maintain context) non-English language subtitled material was excluded from the transcripts as well. Further, I developed a sense of having enough data in order to cover my topic in depth with sufficient cases to fully elaborate on the categories generated. It be can difficult to ascertain limits as to exactly which data to include or exclude in the transcription; as an analysis progresses, additional elements in the footage may surface as somehow relevant (Ratcliff, 2003). LeCompte and Preissle's (1993) insight that "discovering these factors and the interrelationships between them may in fact be one of the purposes of using qualitative methods to begin with" (as cited in Ratcliff, 2003, p. 117). This captured the spirit of my study, as also prescribed by Collier and Collier (1986), who emphasize allowing data to emerge and refining its utility, rather than restricting oneself to predetermined questions and putting constraints on the contexts in which research questions can develop, or limiting deep probing, questioning, and re(en)visioning.

In Phase II codes were generated, categories cross-referenced and, through the process of viewing and comparing thematic foci, films of less compelling or tangential themes were concomitantly eliminated from the sample. The themes that reappeared with greatest regularity, and eventually predictability, emerged from a focus on specific social and political issues. Transcription of films exhibiting characteristics of central themes coincided with the development of greater certainty regarding the issues and questions that would constitute the focus of the study. This process involved simultaneously coding and writing commentary in the margins and facilitated the development of a working thesis which identified negative stereotyping, blaming, and shaming of the other as general discursive moves routinely enacted in constructing anti-immigrant discourse (and accordingly contributing to a larger internally consistent body of discursive representations that fueled further anti-immigration   sentiment).

Once the sample was whittled down to 13 films, coding began. Coding occurred continually "throughout the research process as ideas [were] refined and the understanding of the phenomena change[d]" (Potter, 2003, pp. 83-84). Coding transcripts enabled readily extracting the relevant language samples from the larger corpus (that is, the film or video transcript in its entirety). This "data reduction" was done preliminarily to facilitate ease of analysis once coded categories were ascertained and working operational definitions of the categories were in place. Ultimately, the sample was narrowed to ten films, excluding the three fiction films that had initially been used in the constant comparative process. Table 1 below shows the ten films drawn upon for the final analysis.

Phase III: Interpretive Coding and Constant Comparison

Conducting social research using a grounded theory is purely interpretive work. Its open coding technique gives license to the researcher's own imagination and theoretical sensitivities while adhering to the central analytical principle of constant comparison. Constant comparison involves analysis of the similarities and differences between utterances or segments of text coded along the lines of higher order themes, and the continual "sifting and comparing ... [of] basic data instances, emergent concepts, cases, or theoretical propositions" (Henwood & Pidgeon, 2003, p. 140). This generative, conceptual process is the foundation of the grounded theory method. As texts are subject to scrutiny, codes are identified, notes taken on manuscripts, and memoranda jotted down. This carries on in a continual cycle of refinement resulting in the transformation of raw data into theoretically meaningful resources that eventually reveal the question(s) lying at the heart of the investigation. Memoranda written during this deconstructive and reconstructive process might:

Table 1

Films drawn upon for discourse analysis

Title:

Conquest of Aztlán	2001 Documentary
Los Trabajadores = The Workers	2001 Documentary
New World Border	2001 Documentary
Fear and Learning at Hoover Elementary	1997 Documentary
Go Back to Mexico!	1994 Documentary
Border Brujo	1991 Performance Art
Natives: Immigrant Bashing on the Border	1991 Documentary
Uneasy Neighbors	1989 Documentary
The Lemon Grove Incident	1985 Dramatized Nonfiction
Salt of the Earth	1953 Dramatized Nonfiction

N = 10

"include hunches and insights; comments and samples to be checked out later; and explanations of modifications to or grouping of categories ... means of further stimulating theoretical sensitivity and creativity, generating links to the literature, and [serve] as a vehicle for making public the researcher's emerging theoretical reflections." (Henwood & Pidgeon, 2003, p. 145)

The cyclical process of constant comparison can result in "bipolar contrasts," possibly continua, within categories. The greatest challenge to this approach is "getting out of the maze of detailed and complex codings, deciding on the limits to making constant comparisons, and reaching theoretical closure at integration" (Henwood & Pidgeon, 2003, p. 152).

In order to approach a sense of theoretical closure, once all of the transcripts had been reviewed and coded, they were double-checked and color-coded by core category. By this time discursive instances had been flagged according to Lee, Ottati and Hussain's (2001) and Short and Magaña's (2002) social psychological models (as described in Chapter 2) and the discursive categories of blaming (blue), shaming (yellow), othering (green), and counter-discourse (orange) emerged through an ongoing analysis of the visual and audio texts over repeated viewings.

At this point, stretches of talk bearing any interest whatsoever were copied into electronic archives by code. Extracts were extensively annotated and cross-referenced with relevant or comparable instances across transcripts. In accordance with Wetherell and Potter's (1992) injunction, and with Ratcliff's (2003) suggestion, the selection was inclusive so as to avoid inadvertently excluding content that might later appear impelling or relevant. In some instances codes or categories vanished as they were evaluated to be more usefully subsumed by larger categories, or discursive instances earmarked lost relevance to the greater picture that was continually emerging through the cycle. Table 2), show the codings that represented the end, organic analytical framework.

Additionally, as Wetherell and Potter (1992) advised:

"One of the central elements in analyzing discourse with the aim of identifying interpretive repertoires is to search for variability. Variability is important because it is a signal that different ways of constructing events, processes or groups are being deployed to achieve different effects." (p. 101)

Table 2:

Semantic Taxonomy of Findings: Blaming, Shaming, Othering, and Counter-Discursive Acts

A. Blaming for social ills
  1. Economic problems; stealing jobs and social services
  2. Threatening the status quo; disease; disorder; filth
  3. Crime

B. Shaming the immigrant as inferior
  1. Breaking the law
  2. Inferior values or difference via condescension or humiliation; Immigrant as animal; Immigrant as diseased
  3. Linguistic inferiority

C. Othering: Distancing the immigrant
  1. Us-Them dialectic
  2. Keeping the Other out (e.g. militarization of the border)
D. Counter-discourse
  1. In defense of the migrant worker
  2. Protest as empowerment

In other words, in all phases of a grounded theory/discursive psychological analysis, the researcher should uphold the constructivist worldview that richly informs this kind of interpretive work.

Once the inquiry was well underway, and data continuously subjected to inductive analysis, the pivotal preliminary questions to emerge were: "How and with respect to what social phenomena is blame assigned, implicitly or explicitly, in anti-immigrant expression? To what social processes does this blaming contribute?" Related to the core category of blame were shaming and framing the immigrant as Other. Appropriate questions were formulated as: "How does shaming frame the borderlands immigrant as inferior, and how do these functions serve to permanently frame the immigrant as Other?" Finally, it was deemed necessary to acknowledge the counter-discursive strategies that had manifest alongside the anti-immigrant discourse, in general terms of defense or protestation.

Concluding the Data Discovery

Though the process of grounding a social psychological theory of discourse is informed by the idea that discourse analysis should never reveal conclusive 'results' but rather serve to generate fresh understandings of a body of discursive representations, it was necessary to delineate the 'findings' as answers to the central questions generated. While Charmaz (2004) has suggested that the thickest possible description in applying grounded theory may be obtained by interviewing the social actors under observation, the limited scope of this study precluded pursuing such further endeavor. It remains borne in mind that actors in the film samples should not be construed as wholly representative of general public opinion or any particular subgroup (Henwood & Pidgeon (2003); discursive events are seen phenomenologically. All textual representations of events and issues are polysemic, that is, they are rich with underlying meanings, admixtures of 'truth' and fictional embellishments. By the same token, the language of the actors represents only each particular individual interlocutor's version of truth or worldview.

Using extant video which was constructed purposively to explore and document attitudes towards immigration and to either refute or further anti-immigration agendas, this study in its limited influence contributes to a growing body of literature. The purpose of the research was not to seek out conclusive laws of anti-immigrant discursive behavior, but rather to identify and examine ways in which stereotyping, blaming and shaming express the symbolically unique worldviews of the actors under study, and to present persuasive "exemplars" of these analytical interpretations in the text produced as a result (Lindlof & Taylor, 2002).

Chapter 4

Findings

An analysis of the ten selected film transcripts is discussed below in accordance with the semantic categories which reflect the core codes that emerged during the process of transcript review in Phase II, as shown in Table 2 (Chapter 3, p. 67) and Figure 1 (Appendix B), and in conjunction with the hypothetical constructs offered by the relevant social-psychological literature presented in Chapter 2. The films relay discursive acts of blaming, shaming, and framing the Other, using various rhetorical devices and as justified by arguments characterized by the ideological themes of nativism/ethnicism, obedience to law, or national economic concern. Unique to these data is often explicit or uncensored negative expression. This might be attributable to the candid mood of the interviewing contexts in which the utterances were made (van den Berg, Wetherell, & Houtkoop-Steenstra, 2003; Wetherell & Potter, 1992). Justifications for these negative attitudes are often, ostensibly, attempts at logic which overtly or covertly function to deny racism (Barnes, Palmary, & Durrheim, 2001). Blommaert and Verschueren's (1998) four axes (explicit positive, explicit negative, implicit positive, and implicit negative) are frequently taken into consideration in categorizing these discursive acts. It is found that discursive acts which serve to blame, shame, and frame the immigrant as Other tend to support geopolitical arguments critical of immigrants who cross the Mexican-American boundary unauthorized. The language outwardly expressed by interlocutors represents bipolar ideological extremes and displays social attitudes and opinions on border crossing and the phenomenon of cultural hybridization (Anzaldúa, 1999).

Neat divisions cannot always be made, and there is frequent overlap in the force of these utterances which are at times interwoven and at times somewhat arbitrarily separated in the findings. Throughout the analysis, I bore in mind the questions, "What is happening here? What is taking place in these discursive exchanges, between interlocutors onscreen, between film actors and the interviewer(s), as well as between filmmaker and projected audience-as-interlocutor?" This can be broken down to more pointed research questions as demarcated in broader categories pertaining to blaming, shaming, and Othering the immigrant, and counter-discursive acts.

Blaming the Immigrant as Culpable for Social Ills

The first question put forth in this study asks: How is blaming the immigrant expressed, explicitly and implicitly, among interlocutors who favor the restriction of immigrants' rights with regard to economic problems, disease and disorder, and crime? These are the categories that most frequently surfaced in the film data.

Immigrants are targeted as culpable for pervasive social ills in spite of powerful political and economic forces which provide more plausible explanation. Negative attitudes that inspire blaming are exacerbated during periods of high unemployment (Magaña, 2003). The films *Uneasy Neighbors* (1989), *Natives: Immigrant Bashing* (1991), and *New World Border* (2001) provide copious examples of scapegoating that detracts public attention from locating responsibility for solutions to social problems with the greater powers that be.

Instead, blame is conveniently displaced to those who are largely incapable of self-defense or lack access to a forum which allows opportunities to counter marginalizing stereotypes. A curious byproduct of blaming is that "blaming the other implies a sense of entitlement to humanitarian privileges that the Other does not share" (Lamb, 1996, p. 78). In blaming, one assumes the moral upper hand. In the examples given below, indignation proves to be a form of justification for blaming. The denial of racism (Barnes, Palmary, & Durrheim, 2001) is often provoked concomitantly with the expression of anti-immigrant attitudes, as interlocutors defend the importance of obedience to law, allegiance to the nation-state (i.e., nationalism or nativism), and national economic concern implicitly assumed to be more important than humanitarianism.

Blaming for Stealing Social Services and Jobs

Interlocutors commonly imply that undocumented immigrants are less than fully human and therefore undeserving of precious humanitarian privileges that should be only selectively doled out. Hector Galán's (1994) *Go Back to Mexico!*, a documentary highlighting anti-immigrant sentiment in San Diego County (which borders Mexico), encounters several characters who are explicitly deemed blameworthy, ostensibly for breaking the law (first as trespassers, then as thieves). A conservatively oriented talk radio show hosted by San Diego's former mayor, Roger Hedgecock (who calls himself "a recovering politician") offers a caller ("C") the shelter of anonymity in blatantly expressing negative attitudes toward recent immigrants:

C: If they're here they're breaking the law and they need to leave!

H: ((nodding head in agreement))

C: Five-hundred thousand people get caught coming across our border every year-

H: -that's gotta stop. We don't have enough social services for citizens; for people who deserve it; for people who are sick here in our country. (Galán, 1994)

The caller's imperative injunction suggests that any discussion on whether or not these border crossers should collect social benefits is unwarranted; a black-and-white worldview precludes the admission of arguments in immigrants' favor. Citing the high number of violators bolsters the complaint and prompts Hedgecock to overtake the conversation by emphasizing that immigrants are using limited social service resources meant for people in "our" country. Invoking the possessive reference to "our country" underscores the chasm between deserving and undeserving welfare recipients.

65

While on the one hand, alluding to nameless hordes who, in usurping social services, contribute to the degradation of the quality of life for "deserving" Americans is effective, the personal anecdote functions more effectively to elicit sympathy (Barnes, Palmary, & Durrheim, 2001) as in this exchange between Gary ("G"), a displaced American construction worker and interviewer William Langewiesche ("L"):

G: I went to work for a scaffolding company and I was making seven dollars an hour which was I thought was pretty decent, you know, and they, they let me go, and the reason they let me go was because they could hire two Hispanics to do my work for ten dollars an hour, meaning for both!

L: Gary is unemployed. Like many Americans today, he has been beaten down and has grown bitter at his own country for allowing this to happen. The competition from immigrants seems to him like the most personal of attacks.

G: They're *stealing* and they're not stealing from the government, they're stealing from *me* 'cause I'm the clown that gets unemployed when they're taking my job. They're stealing. They're comin' over here to get *my* job! You know, it's just you might as well come over and get my *house*! You might as well just come over here and starve my *family*! (Galán, 1994)

Gary's anecdote is presumably an honest rendition of his personal experience; from his purview, workers from over the border, clearly an outgroup, are to blame for having undercut the price of his labor. This causes him such humiliation to the extent that Gary self-deprecatingly dubs himself a "clown." Gary does not mention the employer or any other party as culpable, only the migrant workers. News correspondent William Langewiesche, whose periodic injection of sage commentary and lurking presence shape the landscape of this authoritative *Frontline* documentary (hosted by Dan Rather), over-interprets for the audience-interlocutor in stating that the dejected worker Gary blames his country. While Langewiesche may accurately claim that Gary has grown bitter, the bitterness is unmistakably directed at the Other-interloper, not necessarily at "his" country. Gary's anger is geared toward incriminating the vulnerable immigrant; his is a person-blaming ideology (Guimond, Begin, & Palmer, 1989), arguably reductionistic. Gary emphasizes his own humanity and individuality, and defines himself, personally, as the target of "their" shameful theft, regardless of their volition. To Gary, this is indeed a personal matter wherein "talk functions to deflect personal attributions of racism… by positioning the speaker as simply an observer to facts and events rather than a racist bigot" (Barnes, Palmary, & Durrheim, 2001, p. 332). Bearing witness to an observed event is a powerful rhetorical strategy, as no one can deny the truth of Gary's personal experience (i.e., none of us, as audience-interlocutors). However, immediately following these explicitly negative charges, Langewiesche rather condescendingly comments that "Gary sees the world in simple terms, but poses questions that have no easy answers" (Galán, 1994), as if to suggest that Gary were exaggerating the severity of the personal impact the immigrant workers have had on his life circumstances. In fact, Gary does report his subjective experience in lay terms. Though, as Wodak (2001) observed, simplistic notions of conspiratorial activity have little validity in global societies. Langewiesche's interpretation hints at the dilemmatic nature (see Billig, 2001) of the problem plaguing workers just like Gary throughout the borderlands (Lee & Ottati, 2002). Speaking with candor, Gary locates the source of blame within the realm of his immediate experience. Revealing a worldview limited to his personal scope, he impotently challenges a hypothetical – but quite real – nemesis, as follows:

G: (why should I) feed you! I – it's not my problem that their country has a problem! I'm not involved in the politics of their country, you know, I have nothing to do with their country, their county's politics are *their* problems. Not mine. Why do I have to suffer the problems of the politics that are played in their country? (Galán, 1994)

Whether this statement represents Gary's denial of the interrelatedness of economies on an international level (e.g.,

67

the symbiotic shift incurred by NAFTA) or, as Langewiesche suggests, the obtuse simplicity of the layman, the sentiment is nativistic. Apparently Gary is unwilling to entertain a broader, global view of the economy (Borjas, 2004; Feagin, 1997) and prefers to remain within the comfort zone of an us-and-them paradigm.

Another tack is to directly fault the federal government for the upset in the status quo, pitting state against nation. In Paul Espinosa's (1989) *Uneasy Neighbors*, an affluent woman ("W1"), the owner of an expansive ranch property, claims that:

W1: unless we start addressing this as a homelessness issue I don't think we're gonna see a solution. It's a city problem but it's not a city solution. We're talking about federal laws that are governing who's allowed to be here or not allowed to be here ... I think the City Council may, you know, very much have wanted them to say you know, no one may come up here and look for work, but that's not an option the city has. (Espinosa, 1989)

This woman expresses a sense of powerlessness at the local level to oust unwanted squatters from makeshift camps in the canyons of northern San Diego County, and the futility of relying on authorities at the federal level. Another resident ("W2") suggests in the same documentary that the federal government, whose responsibility "keeping them out" is deemed to be, has failed to adequately control its international boundary:

W2: I think it's the government's problem, I think that they should finance it. They didn't put enough people down there to keep them out and they gave them amnesty. I think it's their problem, not ours. (Espinosa, 1989)

The conviction that absolute responsibility is appropriately assigned to the federal government for removing unauthorized immigrants from local territories and advocating stringent federal border patrols inspires citizens to rally around the issue. A heated scene between a passerby, an avid anti-immigrant activist, and a relatively temperate anti-immigrant activist at a crowded street demonstration in the infernal film *Natives: Immigrant Bashing at the Border* (Lerner & Stirling, 1991) captures the depth of mistrust and hostility toward big government:

P: Well the question is do they really to want to control the borders?

A1: I would say no: they [*don't.*]

P: Well! Then ask yourself why: do they *not* want to control the borders?

A1: 'cause: they want the cheap labor: they wanna destroy the unions in America, ah… whatever! (Lerner & Stirling, 1991)

The frustration expressed by the first activist woman ("A1") when confronted by the pedestrian ("P"), whose devil's advocacy helps to unravel her composure, is apparent in the manner in which her voice escalates. She proposes a devious government agenda, insinuating that immigrants threaten and steal the jobs of working people while the government allows it. She then abruptly curtails her train of thought by inarticulately sighing, "ah whatever!" This may indicate an admission, again, of powerlessness facing insurmountably large issues. She may even suspect a more sinister underlying plan. The scene continues as follows with a more aggressive demonstrator ("A2") chiming in:

A2: They're forgetting the American, that's what they're doing, they're not representing *us.* (Lerner & Stirling, 1991)

Once A1 has revealed her suspicion that the U.S. government is conspiring against organized labor ("us" against "them"), A2, a woman carrying an American flag firmly planted over one shoulder, asserts her position: The government is less concerned with the well-being of the average American citizen than with profit-making enterprises.

The exchange continues:

P: Well you send our troops over there to get killed, you need people to come up here to work to pay taxes. Money is money! (Lerner & Stirling, 1991)

Here the man labeled "pedestrian" in the filmmakers' transcript antagonistically implicates the government from a slightly different angle; the government is willing to exploit anyone, his claim implies, regardless of citizenship, for the tax revenues. Demonstrator A2 continues:

A2: They're not payin' taxes though. We're being invaded. That's the big thing and you'd better look around. ((gesticulating angrily)) they can camp on your property!

P: oh no no no

A2: YES they can

P: no they can't.

A2: and there's not a thing you can do about it.

P: there's something you can.

A2: that's the law.

P: that is not the law ... we have a law...

A2: ask: the people in the South Bay. Ask the people in the South Bay and Encinitas and all the canyons. Well, look around in the canyons. They can have their babies over here and they're Americans and they have 'em over here and there's not a thing you can do about it. They go down to the hospital and we pay for them then they get on welfare, they're filling our prisons, they say California is theirs and they're gonna take it back by invading us, so stand up and be American ((turns away in a huff)). (Lerner & Stirling, 1991)

The woman's (A2) loaded tirade begins by blaming the government for its laxity in allowing undocumented immigrants to slip across the border and erode American labor. Ultimately she resorts to proclaiming that the U.S. is being invaded, and that the public is helpless to stop this invasion. The fear of loss of property by invasion, a nativistic appeal to protecting American territory, surfaces elsewhere in the data to represent an extreme reaction to the perception of threat. In continuing with a litany of complaints, A2 covers various bases, including that immigrants' obtaining citizenship represents a threat to national economic security and leads to overcrowding in prisons and hospitals.

The woman's final remark – her ire directed exclusively toward the random passerby who succeeded in provoking her comments – reveals the rationale underlying her position: patriotic fervor. Following a command that he "stand up and be American!" A2 turns away in a huff of disgust; nothing else is to be said. She insinuates that the passerby's questioning the nature of "the problem" is in itself an intolerable stance – "un-American," a blemish of character, one of Goffman's stigmas (1963, as cited in Biernat & Dovidio, 2000). Thereafter, the conversation devolves into a senseless flurry of finger-pointing. The passerby suggests that "solving the problem" should be the goal, rather than name-calling or finger-pointing. However, A2's strategy is to point the finger, blaming the individual who counters her. She displays no sign of openness toward dissecting the nature of the problem or seeking peaceable resolution. Rather, she appears determined to assign blame, to identify a scapegoat, and to ban that scapegoat from the national landscape, as if this is sufficient or viable resolution to "the problem" of illegal immigration:

P: Well the question is, is controlling the border solving the problem? . . . Maybe the solution to the problem is not pre-

A2: -ask your congressman, let's get it solved! They're supposed to represent *us* and they're *not!* And *apathy* is your big problem!

71

P: Lady, instead of attacking *me* attack the problem.

A1: That's why *you're* down here! ((sarcastically, tacitly siding with passerby))

A2: Ha! It's people like *you* that *are* the problem ((laughing smugly to self))

P: Oh! Am I the problem?

A2: You're apathetic, you're un-American. (Lerner & Stirling, 1991)

Questioning how to handle "the problem" is deemed un-American, and rather illogically, apathetic. The demonstrator would seem to deem her protestation of the existence of the problem to be sufficient action and refuses to engage in dialogue about specific solutions.

Blaming the Immigrant for Threatening the Status Quo

When the Other is perceived to threaten the prevailing order of things, or the status quo, blaming is a visceral reaction. Extreme anxiety has been aroused by the threat of the concept of Aztlán, territory of the southwestern U.S. which in 1969 political activists envisioned to be the Aztecan ancestral homeland and, by extension, the Mexican ancestral homeland (Anzaldúa, 1999; Gutiérrez, 1995). Nativists' fear of Mexican migrants plotting to reclaim the U.S. Southwest invoke the threat of the "Plan of Aztlán" to justify an anti- immigrant stance when ethnic ingroup favoritism or nativism are the affective factors motivating the anxiety (Lee, Ottati, & Hussain, 2001). However, the proposition to resist Anglo hegemony and to prevent further cultural assimilation was largely a symbolic act of defiance which helped to foment the Chicano movement, characterized by pride in ethnic identity among young Mexican Americans (Gutiérrez, 1995).

The anti-immigrant group American Patrol / Voices of Citizens Together produced a trilogy of video documentaries, among them *Conquest of Aztlán: The Mexican Takeover of the*

Southwestern U.S. (2001), which, like the others, is devoted to underscoring the threat presented by immigrants.

Debbie, a caller on the radio with Larry Elder, Host of KABC Radio in Los Angeles, had this to say during a June 8, 2001 broadcast:

D: Now it's been a number of years since I've been in Guadalajara, Mexico... while I was down there I learned I studied at one of the universities – sociology professor from the central part of Mexico and they in fact are educating those that are in the outlying villages and towns; umm, they have comic books and they indeed are infiltrating with ideas to come back and take back the entire southwestern part of the United States. There is a really strong movement and people down there do know about it where they're trying to get the [middle] classes in Mexico that you know that they're trying to get all riled up. (Spencer, 2001)

Such propagandistic talk is commonly interpreted as paranoia, and variations on the same theme are repeated throughout the American Patrol's videotapes.

That the status quo never rests so long as unauthorized immigration continues remains justification for nativistic, exclusive attitudes (Lee, Ottati, & Hussain, 2002). In addition to stealing jobs, unsettling the status quo is an even more fundamental and potentially irreversible trend. Resistance to cultural change occurs with each successive wave of nativism (Perea, 1997). "Whether or not the economy can continue to use these people productively," opined Professor Wayne Cornelius of the University of California at San Diego, "the concern is that the culture, the core culture of the United States, whatever that is, has been stretched to the breaking point" (as cited in Galán, 1994). Because of this, some imagine that Americans are a laughingstock among immigrants who take advantage of the U.S.'s dwindling social resources and alter the landscape. For example, in Peek's (2001) *New World Border*, a man commanding the podium at a rally celebrating a new barrier along the U.S.-Mexico boundary complains that:

M:. . . our community orchestras, not enough money; our schools, not enough money. Yet, yet, we promote, we encourage, we've even lured illegal aliens to enter, to stop up, to ignore, to *laugh* at our culture, and to use badly needed resources that'll suck us dry. There's a betrayal, there is a gutless leadership, or both!

Crowd (in unison and scattered voices): *Both! Both!*

Single Voice from crowd: Treason!

M: We rededicate ourselves today not just to the completion of this fence and much more fencing, but we do we dedicate ourselves to the principles that made American great the dream the prize the American citizenship! (Peek, 2001)

The explicitly negative assessment assigns pernicious intent on the part of immigrants "to suck us dry," quite a stretch juxtaposed with immigrants' reported modest perception of earning enough money to provide basic subsistence for families in spite of the pain caused by separation (Annerino, 1999; Courtney, 2001; Galán, 1994; Nava & Thomas, 1984). The speaker (again) alludes to the nation-state's betrayal of allegiance to its native citizens, jabbing below-the-belt by taunting it a "gutless leadership."

One of the most harrowing threats to the status quo, to the monocultural illusion of happiness, is the noticeable filth, disease, or "Third World" atmosphere created by impoverished, unwanted immigrants. A sample from Lerner and Stirling's (1991) *Natives: Immigrant Bashing at the Border* demonstrates how this fear is escalated to hyperbole:

A2: they bring dis*ease* in here, we've got outbreaks of diseases that have been un- under control for years! All of these illegal aliens coming in here have caused our diseases to sky rocket!

P: ((shruggingly)) I don't know what the evidence of diseases is. (Lerner & Stirling, 1991)

The complaint that immigrants carry disease is a significant factor in the battle for school segregation as depicted in Espinosa's (1985) *The Lemon Grove Incident*. The docudrama poignantly reenacts events which took place from 1930 to 1931 in the community near San Diego. The film depicts the school environment as a training ground for learning one's rightful place in the social hierarchy as pertains to native language and ethnicity. In the opening scene, the Lemon Grove School board members are meeting to discuss removing the Mexican children to a separate school. Interlocutors cite a hodgepodge of justifiable reasons, among them, "overcrowding" and the lack of English language proficiency among Mexican children:

C ((smiling graciously)): As secretary of the Lemon Grove Parent-Teachers' Association, I have been asked to approach the school board with the following request: Whereas we, members of the Lemon Grove PTA, deem that an emergency has arisen at the Lemon Grove grammar school, we request that the school board establish a separate school for the Mexican children of this district. We feel that such a school has become a necessity due to a severe situation of overcrowding in present classrooms. Furthermore, the Mexican children are deficient in their knowledge of the English language, causing their classmates to learn at a much slower rate. A separate school would also improve the general situation of sanitation and morals in the school which has been deteriorating. We respectfully ask that the school board consider action on this petition immediately.

M1: Thank you Claire.

M2: ((nodding in agreement)) Well, I can speak for the Chamber of Commerce; we would back the idea. From what I've heard there are just too many kids in that school. Now I understand that last week the toilets backed up?

M3: Well, it's not the first time it's happened.

M2: The Chamber is planning a big promotion right now with

75

advertisements from the newspaper and lots of publicity. If we want to bring new people here I think we've got to have a separate school for the Mexicans.

Lady: I thought we were taking care of the Mexican problem with Catherine Ellie's class. Doesn't she teach most of them now?

M3: Look, Catherine Ellie doesn't have all the Mexicans anymore; the older ones are movin' out of her class!

C: Last year, the members of the PTA went to each of their homes, we wanted to take their children to the dentist. Lord knows, we tried to impress upon the mothers the importance of common cleanliness. ((voice breaking)) Well, they've got so many kids! And if there's a stick of furniture in any of the rooms, it's a surprise. Most of the boys just run around barefoot. Heaven only knows what diseases they're bringing back to school. (Espinosa, 1985)

Claire ("C") assigns blanket blame to the Mexican children for degrading the quality of the Lemon Grove School, with multiple excuses: overcrowding, insufficient English ability, disrupting the pace of learning for all students, poor sanitation, poor moral values. As deviants, they should forever remain stigmatized outsiders (Falk, 2001). In this instance blaming doubles with shaming, by insulting the children and their families. Fault for problems with the plumbing automatically being attributed to the Mexicans evokes an unkind somatic metaphor which elsewhere has been used to refer to the inhabitants south of the border (Fox, 1999). Here too, "it's not the first time it's happened." Later, under oath, Andy Anderson ("AA"), chair of the Lemon Grove school board, testifies to the Supreme Court in a case brought against the Board by the Mexican families that:

L: And Mr. Anderson, you were also concerned with overcrowding, were you not?

AA: Ah: yes sir, we had a real emergency situation here! Ah, there's simply too many kids in that school: why the toilets were backin' up on us last month! (Espinosa, 1985)

Toilets backing up may seem a legitimate, concrete complaint, but assigning blame to the Mexican population – the excess, the Other, only barely disguises the speaker's prejudice (Lee, Ottati, & Hussain, 2001).

Proposed segregation is tantamount to instilling a kind of internal barrier, the official purpose of which is to improve conditions for the non-Mexican children, in that they will no longer be tainted by exposure to the Mexicans, the school board's chief concern. Another main thrust behind segregation is to 'hide' the "Mexican problem" from public view; the Chamber of Commerce is currently soliciting visitors to the city and does not wish to highlight the presence of its unsightly Mexican underclass – in spite of the city's dependency on their agricultural labor for its growth. Yet none of this can be stated up front when the case goes to court. Situated behind closed doors, however, Claire's bold accusations of lack of "common cleanliness" and oblique allusion to hypersexuality ("so many kids"), together with her tacit disapproval of the Mexican families' sparsely furnished homes and rampant barefoot boys (read: lack of control) all serve to justify her charge that the Mexican children are apt to infect the school with disease (Nevins, 2002; Santa Ana, 2002; Short & Magaña, 2002). To the speaker's mind, these characteristics are proof of values which oppose those of the Anglo majority. As Ramirez (1988) noted, "[t]he values ascribed to Mexican-Americans are viewed as negative and, by virtue of the terms that are used to label these values, as completely opposite to those of the dominant cultural group" (p. 139). Espousing these different values is regarded as ample justification for segregation (Dockett & North-Schulte, 2003).

Later on in the film, the court testimony of Miss Markland, a first-year teacher at the school, reinforces this attitude of difference as inferiority to justify segregation.

L1: Miss Markland would you simply: describe what you have

seen in the Mexican homes.

MM: Their homes have no books, magazines, or even newspapers. The only time English is spoken is at school ((turns to look at judge)). Since health and sanitation are problems in their homes it's only natural that they have difficulties concentrating on school. I feel that the Americanization school will improve their lives. (Espinosa, 1985)

Illiteracy and poverty are viewed by Miss Markland as intractable problems. What is perceived as substandard cleanliness is deemed cause for the students being behind their peers. In the following passage, while Miss Markland denies that she holds prejudices, she contradictorily admits to a belief in unequal potentials as an unalterable truth due to the origins of the children during this interrogation while on the witness stand:

M: They've started this new school so that the Mexican students will not feel embarrassed about the superior abilities of their classmates. You see in this way the Mexican children will not develop feelings of inferiority.

L2: And you can say without a doubt that the Mexican students are behind in their studies.

M: Absolutely. I could go down the list of Mexican children in class and tell you just how far behind each of them is. Uh Roberto Ruiz is a year behind. Jesus Benir is two years, Robert Alvarez is a year, [x x] is a year, and Frances Romero is two years behind.

L2: Miss Markland, do you have any prejudices against the Mexican people?

M: No. No I do not ((shaking head sideways emphatically)). Now I believe that this Americanization school was built with the interest of the Mexican children in mind. They'll be taught the language, the customs, and the culture of this country. You have to realize that most of these children come from homes where ignorance and poverty prevail. (Espinosa, 1985)

Miss Markland feigns concern for the Mexican children in stating that "…the Mexican children will not develop feelings of inferiority" by relocating to a separate school. The genuineness behind this remark is questionable; as Crawford (2000) would contend, the Lemon Grove School Board's likely covert agenda is to stunt diversity and multiculturalism via segregation rather than to protect the children's feelings of difference.

Nearly 70 years later in Los Angeles in *Fear and Learning at Hoover Elementary* (Simón, 1997) similar attitudes are revealed. Diane, a non-Spanish-speaking teacher who voted in favor of Proposition 187 ("Di"), claims that family values which oppose those of the dominant majority are the source of the problem of poor school performance:

Di ((extremely rapid speech)): It sounds awful but I've been at Hoover for seven years and I think the children are getting worse and worse not better I blame the families. I think the family needs to say 'you will go to college, what did you do for homework? What did you do in school today? School is important.' It's not somewhere where you go to be babysat and play, it's somewhere where you go to learn. (Simón, 1997)

Whether or not divergent values will ever be reconciled and the status quo reclaimed is a moot point since the steady arrival of immigrants from south of the border shows no sign of abating (de la Garza & DeSipio, 1998). Diane divulges her sense of intolerance and impatience for difference, a sense of frustration with the atmosphere of flux which, in Nhât Hanh's (2003) ontology, is inescapable. This penchant for values judgment is discussed at greater length below in terms of shaming by framing the immigrant as inferior.

Blaming Immigrants for Crime
Crime is a frequently voiced concern for which the unauthorized immigrant takes the rap; in anti-immigrant

discourse, inherent in the dubious nature of his method of entering the U.S. he poses a menace to public safety (Nevins, 2002). Having broken the law grants interlocutors permission to negatively construct 'intruders.' Cause for labeling any one representative of the outgroup as a criminal psychologically facilitates attaching the label to other members of the same ethnic group (Short & Magaña, 2002). This is evident in a *vox populi* (i.e., voice of the people) succession strung together by Espinosa (1989), in which the first voice claims:

"We've had two-and-a-half years of hell! And there was about forty, fifty of them living out here! We ne- we couldn't even step out our door at night," followed by "Why should a lady have to call her councilwoman to tell her there are men that are uh that come into her backyard and steal her fruit and defecate and burglarize the house."

This latter claim, in particular, in content and in tone, betrays evidence of anger that the problem should be infringing on her life at all. The violation of hygienic commonsense values alluded to is frequently likened to the encroachment of "Third World" living standards. Clearly, this is an unwanted symbiosis. As the omniscient narrator of *Uneasy Neighbors* informs the audience:

The living conditions here resemble what Americans expect only in the third world. Shelters of plywood and plastic are for the lucky ones. Others live under bushes or in these so-called spider holes. For months, even years at a time, they go without the basic necessities most Americans take for granted – running water, toilet, and electricity. The increasing visibility of these camps right next to affluent neighborhoods raises troubling questions. Can the rich look the other way while the poor who contribute to this wealth live in desperate conditions? Can the community exist when two groups face such different realities? Is there any alternative to living side by side as uneasy neighbors. (Espinosa, 1989)

The narration is an attempt to explain the revulsion to the Other and to the forced conditions of co-existence and unwanted symbiosis. Camp dwellers are blamed for spoiling a once-pristine atmosphere and altering the status quo. Numerous anecdotes echo this concern. As Deann, an affluent horse rancher of North San Diego County, opined in *Go Back to Mexico!*:

Dean: we do have problems with um illegal ah laborers who work up here live up here; um some of them drive their cars on the roads erratically. They uh there's just a number of problems here associated with living here and sharing my home and my area with people I feel don't really belong here. I've decided to take a stand. My husband and I talked about it and we decided that what we were doing; hiring them was contributing to the problem that was why they were coming here, and so we stopped hiring them and so even though now there are those with green cards I refuse to hire them because I don't want to contribute to the problem that we have in this state. (Galán, 1994)

The amnesty provided by Immigration Reform and Control Act (IRCA) in 1986 (Ono & Sloop, 2002) is insufficient entitlement to residency in Deann's worldview; however, the Others still do not belong. The problem lies not in the legal status of these immigrants, but in what the speaker perceives to be an untenable symbiosis. Belonging is the issue at stake, and she cannot reconcile "them" as a part of "us." Others' erratic habits upset the status quo; Deann is psychologically attached to having recognized difference in the Other (Dockett & North-Schulte, 2003). As the narrator of *Uneasy Neighbors* (1989) suggests, the worlds of the two groups are so disparate that side-by-side living seems impossible.

A similar sentiment is echoed by Jenna, a young mother and featured voice in opposition to a proposed day labor site in her in Austin, Texas neighborhood:

J: They had concerns that they were being thought of as, as, these horrible people and uh I spoke to ah day laborers specifically to tell them NO, that's not the problem. The problem is that we're worried about what *could* happen, it's not *you*. It could be one day, one person comes in, and they're not truly a day laborer, and yet they're here on the site. And it just takes one time, one child, one woman, one person, being hurt by the center to make the center go downhill or completely fail. (Courtney, 2001)

In the example given, the speaker attempts to correct the indirect implication that the criminal behavior of the Other ("these horrible people") is feared by depersonalizing: "It's not you." This remark conveys that she is instantly aware that her protest of the day labor site contradicts her words. She attempts to bridge that gap, and to distance herself from the force of this discursive act by conjecturing into the future, using the modal "could" to suggest that concerns were merely hypothetical. In fact, quite possibly she had been thinking

"...at least fleetingly – that they were "these horrible people." Here Jenna betrays the "NIMBY" (i.e., 'Not In My Back Yard') mentality that is prevalent when residents are overwhelmed by an unwanted change encroaching upon their territory. Jenna is clinging to a stereotype that guides her expectations, a diversion from attending to individuating information that is directly before her as evidence, explain Biernat and Dovidio (2000): "[S]tereotypes shape interpretations ... [and] guide expectations and inferences in systematic ways," serving to perpetuate prejudice (p. 98). Even further, Jenna exhibits sympathy toward the Other by suggesting that she is partly opposed to the center's relocation to her neighborhood because of the risk of its going "downhill." Nevertheless, she expresses zero tolerance for deviance in warning that "...it takes just one time, one child, one woman, one person, being hurt by the center to make the center go downhill or completely fail." The speaker attempts to mitigate and disguise the accusatory force of her statement by indicating that the center, an inanimate object, could hurt someone. In fact, she is framing the stigmatized members of the group likely to hang out at the center as a symbolic threat." (Stangor & Crandall, 2000).

The argument that predominantly criminal elements are

penetrating the international boundary has gained momentum and been hyped up by mainstream news media since the terrorist attacks of September 11, 2001, providing persuasive rationale for increasing Border Patrol crackdowns. Even prior to the events of 9/11, criminal violence was frequently cited as justification for border vigilantism. Muriel Watson ("M"), founder of San Diego's citizen action group *Light Up the Border*, made the following statement:

M: I have been watching uh you know because that what's brought me down here was the violence and what have you and the murders and there and, and, I said hey, enough's *enough*, so that's when we started Light Up, to counteract that! And ah, ah, I have seen ah a good slow down on-on that kind of violence and that's-that was the point. (Lerner & Stirling, 1991)

Whether Muriel's vigilant eyewitness account ("I have been watching") of a slowdown in violence in the borderlands is factual or not is contestable. The *Los Angeles Times* has consistently reported that neither vigilantism nor recent Border Patrol crackdowns have significantly alleviated violence or unauthorized border crossings (Alonso-Zaldivar, 2005), though they note that California Governor Arnold Schwarzenegger would credit the former with deterring unauthorized crossers in the case of the Arizona Minuteman Project (Gorman, 2005). The San Diego Border Patrol chief himself admitted that *Light Up the Border* functioned mainly to quell residents' trepidations about uncontrolled border traffic (Lerner & Stirling, 1991).

Violent acts committed by or against the "illegal" border crosser are not the only concern; the issue points back to overcrowding and the costs of imprisoning people, as evidenced by this conversation between Davida ("D") and Harry ("H") while they weed their lawn:

D: Look, son, go over to the jail in San Diego; find out how many illegal kids are in there, how many illegals are there. I bet you seventy-five percent of our jails are filled with illegals that

have committed crimes. You don't have to come and ask me about it, you know? I mean are you so naïve that you don't believe-
H: -why don't they charge the Mexican government room and board for these people that they put in jail over here... They'd see that the people don't come over the border-((smiling to self as if clever))

D: They won't -oh no! *Mexico* don't give a damn.

H: I say if they would make Mexico put-pay room and board for the Mexicans that are put in jail the illegals... Uh, then the Mexican government would keep them in their own country to save money ((laughter))

D: Well you see most of the-so many of them I don't know what percentage of people are of a, a, less ah, ah, intellectually. Let's say they don't even recognize a zero because its round that's what I say but they can sure come and rip off Medicare and even some even some doctors that have just come from come from um foreign countries. (Espinosa, 1989)

The criminal label here is liberally applied to all "illegals" (Nevins, 2002) and the facts cited are vague. Davida readily accuses the filmmaker of being naïve, then, ironically, ineloquently proceeds to attack the mentality of the Mexican people, unable to finish her sentence. The two reveal that they are ill-informed on the issue, with Harry dreaming up a scenario wherein Mexico foots the bill for its citizens housed in American jails, a negotiation which in fact is impossible.

Another aspect of criminality is that it is etching away at the commonplace aesthetics of a landscape to create what interlocutors regularly liken to a Third World atmosphere. This is a telltale sign of association with crime and drugs, as Winnie ("W") explains while accompanying the filmmakers on a driving tour of a downtrodden area:

W: you don't have a problem, you do not see the walls all wrote on... Okay? Right there ((gesturing with head toward right)) illegal aliens and drugs was at that house police broke it up… Right round the corner didn't show you cuz I couldn't. Ah, illegal aliens was a [drop] house right across the street from my church. I live in a neighborhood you would have to see it you'd be surprised what you see… And the [back] alleys be [full], we never saw cars on the street and fixin' like you saw here and since they over whether they illegal or *not* they have carried down the neighborhood I put it like that, that's sitting on the street which is illegal right there. We don't have a police force to take care of it if you notice. (Lerner & Stirling, 1991)

Winnie is equally as obsessed with parking aberrations as she is with graffiti – she is depicted scouring the neighborhood for infractions of the law and of commonplace aesthetic values. Yet such scouts on the lookout for illegal activity, however innocuous, may in part be responsible for filling up the crowded jails they complain about by constantly alerting police.

Further, in the above passage, Winnie is indicting all immigrants. The immediate negative association of immigrants with crime and drugs spreads rampantly in the anti- immigrant discourse and functions to reproduce expectations of the association, or exaggerations of the 'illegal' activity. A fellow identified as Bob suggests while chatting with Muriel, another man, and a Border Patrol officer at a San Diego border checkpoint:

Bob: -but supposedly now in San Diego: misdemeanors don't go to jail anymore as felons-felonies so anybody in the jail are felons… and maybe forty to fifty percent are ((breaking into laughter)) illegal aliens so we have to turn some of our criminals loose early because there are, are, not enough beds available and so that's, that's, another impact of people coming over in such large numbers, in the process they're performing burglaries, auto thefts, um, you know, I need to say drug dealing. (Lerner & Stirling, 1991)

As Bob paints a picture of mayhem, his line of logic

disintegrates. It may be the case that many housed in jails are immigrants who crossed the border illegally; however, again, here is another discursive attempt to extend the criminal label to all immigrants by virtue of their having crossed the border unauthorized.

Shaming: Framing the Immigrant as Inferior

The second question this study asks is: What role does shaming play in framing the borderlands immigrant as inferior with respect to breaking the law, values, difference, and language status as a non- or non-native English speaker?

Pejorative labels function as tools for shaming. Take, for example, the word 'illegal' as a modifier of the noun 'alien' or 'immigrant,' which appears to be employed as appropriate terminology in mainstream discursive venues such as the *Los Angeles Times* as well as overtly right wing publications such as the *Middle American News*. As a noun, the word 'illegal,' in its singular form, and 'illegals,' in plural, have become widely used stigmatic labels in informal discourse, which effectively marginalizes, devalues, and dehumanizes the Other in aiming to construct the image of a singular enemy (Fairclough, 1989). The use of 'illegal' as a noun has also been adopted as standard terminology among government officials in disseminating political rhetoric. Informal labeling of this kind has far more potent effects on the everyday lives of everyday citizens than formal labeling (Falk, 2001).

As if being labeled a criminal or 'an illegal' is not insult enough, resembling a suspect phenotype also puts one at risk of harassment. In *The Unwanted* (Ruiz & Del Olmo, 1975) the camera follows immigration officers approaching various men who appear to be Latino, interrogating them as to their birthplace. Many cite American locations. This phenomenon forms the premise of the fiction film *Born in East L.A.* (Marin & MacGregor, 1998), in which the chief protagonist, a lifelong Angeleno, is mistakenly deported to Tijuana on the basis of his appearance. (Neither of these two films were drawn upon for this analysis, though they both address issues relevant to the themes explored.)

Shaming for Breaking the Law

One message that was repeatedly conveyed in the analysis of the ten films, often by vox populi, was that unauthorized immigrants should be ashamed of themselves for breaking the law. The vox populi (or vox pop) is a frequently used device in documentary which functions to condense the giving of a diversity of opinions into a rapid series of voices which deliver a salient message, or to set up a dialectic between contradictory points on an issue (Rabiger, 1987). The repetitive nature of vox pop makes it an effective rhetorical tool for reinforcing and reproducing ideology. This example is a vox pop snippet situated at the opening of the film *Go Back to Mexico!* (Galán, 1994), setting the stage for reverberating similar sentiments throughout the remainder of the film:

Man: I frankly don't care why they come... If they're here they're breaking the law of the United States and they need to leave. (Galán, 1994)

As noted with regard to blaming (recall the radio caller's near-identical injunction that "if they're here they're breaking the law and they need to leave"), such explicitly negative anti-immigrant talk indicates that by virtue of being law-breakers the issues is precluded from discussion. Other factors warrant no consideration; this is a black-and-white issue based on an unquestioned ideological assumption (Billig et al., 1988; Billig, 2001; Lamb, 1996). Diane, a longtime teacher at Hoover Elementary School, frankly supports the same view after pondering aloud the delicacy of her position as a teacher being pressured to comply with Proposition 187 by reporting the children of undocumented immigrants in her classroom:

Di: I don't want to be kicking my students out of the class. I'm not going to say oh you're illegal. I don't want to be a rat, but then again too the schools are overcrowded. Teachers are taking a pay cut we don't have enough money to put all these kids in school if they don't belong there they shouldn't be there I voted yes on 187. I didn't vote on yes as a personal issue. I voted for the broad spectrum that we're just running out of money, we can't take care of everyone and people need to know you can't come here and break a law. (Simón, 1997)

Diane's rapid-fire diatribe touches upon the dilemmatic nature of the problem (Billig et al., 1988). On the one hand, she does not wish "to be a rat." On the other hand, she claims that there is not enough money to support the kids who "shouldn't be there," a situation which audience-interlocutors are to understand puts Diane in a no-win position. She appeals to the film audience to elicit its sympathy for her difficult position, reasoning that children of undocumented immigrants should not be at Hoover Elementary School because they fit into the disdainful law-breaker category. Ultimately Diane presents her stance as a black-and-white issue, justifying her unwavering stance in support of Proposition 187 by deferring to the law.

Later in the film, Diane reappears, having asked the filmmaker, Laura ("L"), to return so that she might clarify her position.

L: This time, Diane asked to talk to us.

Di: ((sitting with legs crossed on desktop, talking extremely fast)) I've never been a racist, I have never judged people on what they looked like on the outside, what they look like on the inside, but I thought about the issues we talked about last night, and 187, the riots and things like that, and. What I said taken out of context or even in context could sound like I'm kinda hard line and I don't feel I am, and I wanted you to come back, so I could kind explain myself so that I'm understood, not misunderstood. And umm: I guess um most of the issues are, you know, this job, and yesterday Laura mentioned that there's teachers that don't feel I should be here. And I disagree with that I feel like I should be here 'cause I care about the kids. But the bottom line for me ((chopping side of hand emphatically on other hand)) with 187 is that it's a law and I don't feel people should break the law. I have always followed the law, I have never been in trouble with the law. (Simón, 1997)

Diane's final remark reveals that she holds others to her own standards, and she justifies her position by touting her own record as a non-lawbreaker. She opens by dismissing an anticipated charge of racism and, in spite of her firm stance, disengages herself from responsibility for her verbal actions in saying "What I said taken out of context or even in context could sound like I'm kinda hard line and I don't feel I am." She stresses her concern for the children, a point which, based on her vote in favor of Proposition 187, is easily open to refutation. Following Lee, Ottati, and Hussain's (2001) hypothesis, obeying the law is a matter of principle in Diane's perspective. Those who do not uphold this principle are implicitly shamed for lack of appropriate values.

An implicit message being sent by those to whom obeying the law is strictly a matter of principle is that, regardless of law-breakers' reasons, they do not deserve the same respect as those who comply with the law. Community members who are perceived to facilitate the influx of unauthorized immigrants, as represented in *Uneasy Neighbors* (Espinosa, 1989), are as also shunned as law-breakers:

W: Definitely the people in the community that hire illegal or undocumented people to do yard work and housework and so on are contributing to the problem . . .

This remark made by an affluent resident, accuses other community members of being complicit with law-breaking behavior and functions to demarcate more sharply the chasm between the good and the bad, or us and them, into opposing moral camps. To contribute to the already unwieldy problem of illicit migrant workers camping in the canyons by eagerly exploiting their cheap labor encourages the workers to camp behind the exclusive homes and is cause for shame (Nevins, 2002).

In their inherent immorality law-breakers are deemed fair game for the hurling of insults. Placards being paraded by anti-immigrant activists in the film *New World Border* (Peek, 2001) claim that "illegal aliens are welfare leeches" and implore

89

"what part of illegal don't you understand?" In their convictions of immigrants' immorality, anti-immigrant activists presume moral superiority over the inferior "invaders" (Spencer, 2001; see also the Web site of *Americans for Immigration Control, Inc.* at www.immigrationcontrol.com).

Shaming for Values or Difference via Condescension and Humiliation

Shaming commingles closely with blaming. As established, immigrants are frequently blamed for degrading the environment (Nevins, 2002). At the same time, such blaming talk implicitly functions to shame the immigrant for having 'inferior' cultural values which, like law-breaking, is treated as evidence of inherent immorality or inferiority. In the next extract, while meticulously weeding the lawn, Davida ("D") expresses her incredulity at this presumed inferiority, followed by a cut to Winnie ("W"), who reinforces Davida's complaint:

D: The thing is that sometimes gripes me too is that they come here and they don't even learn to to to learn to keep their yards clean or nothing they may not be doing-have a, any, job or anything but they're just sitting around picking yer fleas off o' their the dogs ((breaks into slightly nervous laugh)) back or whatever, y' know?

W: Everywhere they go they tear up the community… cars in the lawn not supposed to be placed there they (add on) when they get here you go through an alley and all you see hangin' out mostly is, is, people you *know* is illegal aliens, you know, *yes*! that's what I would say it's been in the newspaper. It just came out last week, which we been knowin' but they don't want you to touch it: How they drain the system, how they don't come over to be: our citizens. Did you read in the paper where they go to San Diego High they come over here to learn how to speak English and go back and say well we'll go back and get us a business- you wanna turn here please make a, ah, left right here? (Lerner & Stirling, 1991)

Davida, in the midst of laboring over her lawn, derides the

Other for not similarly prioritizing such activity. She regards her "gripe" as legitimate in that the behavior she condemns conflicts with her own commonsense values (Billig, 2001). In implying that failing to share the same aesthetic values is shameful, Davida insinuates cultural inferiority. Such implied decree gives further license to allude to immigrants' perceived laziness and to allege that they would rather engage in the filthy, lowly practice of picking fleas off their dogs. The filmmakers reinforce this judgment in cutting to Winnie, whose driving tour provides proof to both the filmmakers and to the audience-interlocutors of Mexican immigrants' shameful defiling of the urban landscape. "[T]hey tear up the community" by littering and loitering, announcing their presence. In addition to these aesthetic violations, Winnie's charge of usury – that is, immigrants cross the international boundary to take advantage of its resources – also carries the implicitly negative illocutionary force of shaming for immoral behavior. Shaming for difference, it can be surmised, is a reaction to immigrants' representing a threat to the status quo.

Framing immigrants as liars is another way of shaming them for immorality. Loren ("L"), a boat repairman, laments that U.S. social services are being taken advantage of by immigrants:

L: If you're an illegal alien and you go into our county welfare offices you can get welfare, they say 'where do you live' 'I live here' ah 'where's your papers?' 'ah I don't have 'em I lost em' ah ' what's your name?' ah and you make up a name and they give you money! (Galán, 1994)

This statement is comparable to Gary's charge that immigrants steal jobs (see above). Both express concern about their survival. Charges of lying and theft can be interpreted as indirect attempts to humiliate the immigrant for having even imposed complications in others' lives.

Another extract from *Fear and Learning at Hoover Elementary* (Simón, 1997), which probes attitudes about California's Proposition 187, is illustrative, because it shows an adult interlocutor ("P") attempting to humiliate schoolchildren for morally unacceptable behavior:

P: You know I've been in this country all my life, and I've lived in cities, and I've lived in a lot of different cities in a lot of different places, and (.) you walk up and down these streets in Los Angeles, you find people that don't take time to go to the bathroom, you find all kind of trash on the street, I can go to all different cities around, and some of 'em aren't as bad as Los Angeles is in that respect! I will not throw a chewing gum wrapper on the ground, I was taught when I was growing up that we had to take care of the land.

G: Are you saying that we do?

P: I'm saying that somebody does, if you don't believe me go out to the sidewalk out on the street

G: well I know, I know people who-

B:-Americans do that too

G: I know

P: I didn't say, I didn't say-

G: every kind of people

P: I didn't say any kind of people, I'm just saying what is happening that didn't use to happen

G: I think you're saying that just because

P: no, you're interpreting it that way, you're interpreting it that way

G: just because people from another country's coming because you, you, just said that American people, before we weren't here, they didn't do that. I mean that you're saying that, all of us, that are that are legal do-

P: -who walks up and down the streets out here? All, all of us

G: who throws trash on the streets out here?

B1: all of us

B2: everybody

P: no I don't!

B: but American people do too

P: I don't say it's not Americans too but I'm saying I don't! it's my country I'm living in, and I want it to stay nice!

B: it ain't yours, it's everybody's!

P: I say it's my country that I'm living in! (Simón, 1997)

This passage is extraordinary in that Mr. Pietermayer has the gall to directly confront the assembled group of children with the implication that local immigrants have degraded the environment. Aside from the truth value of this charge, he seems to be indicting the entire community, which puts the children on the defensive. Highlighting shameful transgressions with the expectation that 'public' exposure will reform the perceived transgressors may be Pietermayer's preferred way of educating. However, the sole female child in the group reminds Mr. Pietermayer that the issue under discussion is one of legality, thereby indirectly exposing the racist undertones of his accusation. When she requests clarification (". . . you're saying that, all of us, that are legal . . ."), he cuts her off with the antagonistic question, "who walks up and down the streets out here?" as if the answer is evident. In responding as such, Mr. Pietermayer strays further from the issue, as if immigrants' littering is sufficient support to exclude children from school.

Mr. Pietermayer is surely emboldened in this explicit, face-to-face condescension because his interlocutors are only children and he is permitted to authoritatively dominate them. He is deliberately attempting to cause the children to feel shame for belonging to the outgroup that violates mainstream social norms (Smith et al., 2002). However, condescension to the immigrant Other frequently occurs with adults as well. The following example from *Salt of the Earth* (Biberman, Jarrico, & Wilson, 1954), a true story which chronicles the uprising of miners in New Mexico (a number of whom are not immigrants but Native Americans), exemplifies condescension to the adult as if he is an infantile being. In the selected scene, striking miners are blocking the passage of the company president's vehicle. The exchange involves the boss ("B"), his male passenger ("M"), Ramón, the picket captain ("R"), and another miner on strike ("S"):

P: Well are they gonna let us pass?

B: Eventually. This is just a little ritual to impress us with their power.

R: ((to striking miners, jokingly, sarcastically, smiling)) Now why don't you let this gentleman pass! Don't you know who's in that car?

S: [x x x x]

R: No, no! It's the president of the company himself. Coming all the way over here to make [Jenkins] general manager!

Group: ((bursts out in laughter))

P: Childish.

B: Well they're like children in many ways. Sometimes you have to humor them, sometimes you have to spank them, *some*times you have to take their food away. Well here comes the one that we're talking about. He's quite a character. ((Hmm!)) Claims his grandfather once owned the land where the mine is now ((hmm!)). (Biberman, Jarrico, & Wilson, 1954)

The boss's likening the adult men to children relegates them to an inferior rank. His admonitions that they must be treated like children belies a fundamental lack of respect and condescension, the implication being that these childlike miners do not deserve the considerations ordinarily accorded to a full-fledged adult.

Humiliation, making one feel as if one's worth is somehow less than that of others, or as if one does not satisfy ingroup criteria, is commonly the goal and the outcome of this kind of talk (Brothers, 2005; hooks, 1994). When probed by Laura, the filmmaker, the children participating in the roundtable discussion at Hoover Elementary School plainly state the emotional impact of being condescended to:

L: Among you guys, do you know what the word illegal means? Illegal alien?

Kids: Yes. – Yeah.

L: How does that word make you feel? What does it mean?

Boy B: Uh, I feel like when they call us illegal aliens that they calling us like, like, we're not human beings, like we're just ah a little piece of dirt or something, like we wanna feel like human beings, like Americans too.

Boy C: [x x x]

Boy A: They treat us like if we're enemies. Like if we're their enemies or something. (Simón, 1997)

That in order to earn human being status, one must be an American, not a "piece of dirt" immigrant, is a poignant and honest statement. When Boy A says that "they treat us like if we're their enemies," the sting he feels at being stigmatized as an 'illegal' immigrant, and shamed for it, is evident. This concept of the immigrant as the enemy Other is further illustrated with examples in a forthcoming section on Othering.

Shaming also occurs when people talk about the immigrant as if diseased, or as if an animal. In the next excerpt, Harry ("H") and Davida ("D") allege that:

H: The Mexican people don't know what democracy is about, they are a people who are illiterate to a great extent, if not completely illiterate, and it's hard to explain things to people-

D:-no because the poor people are not interested in politics!

H: They don't have the background, the educational background to understand what you're trying to do for them.

D: No, and then they breed like, like, rabbits, putting it mildly.

H: Yeah well y' know that's the solution.

D: You know they have they have no conception of ah of thinking how am I going to how am I gonna feed this child how am I gonna edu*cate* it. Oh, there's a good ol' gringo, he will pay for it because we're a we're a compassionate nation

[...]

D: it looks like a third world country.

Davida's animal simile ("they breed like . . . rabbits") is a means of relegating immigrants to subhuman status. Tacking on "putting it mildly" to intensify her claim is a way of defending her hyperbolic estimation. Animal metaphors are commonly used in both extreme anti-immigrant and mainstream discourse in referring to immigrants as a tactic for creating distance, stigmatizing, or Othering (Santa Ana, 2002). In Davida's worldview, the real human being, the "good ol' gringo," ever the custodian of the helpless animal, belongs to a "compassionate nation." However, by scorning compassion, Davida unwittingly dissociates herself from that compassionate nation of which she is a 'native.'

An indirect equation of Mexicans with animals is exemplified by this snippet from *New World Border* (Peek, 2001), at an anti-immigrant rally in which brash name-calling appears to be a tactic for shaming the immigrant. To the crowd at large, one man yells:

Man: *Who's the real weapon!* ((pointing and jabbing at the air aggressively)) *Mestizos go back to the swamps and jungles of your country!*

The command that Mestizos return to their swamps and jungles, a place hospitable only to animals who fester and prowl in its murkiness, is an indirect strategy for relegating the human beings to lowly 'animal' status.

Just as debasing as the animal metaphor is the implicit dehumanization of the Mexican migrant worker as a diseased or objectionable object, as in this court hearing with the City Council of Austin, Texas, where citizens unite to oppose the relocation of a day center for migrant workers:

C1: My neighborhood association by the way which is not a very established neighborhood association found out about this on the *news*! No city official came to *my* door. No city official ((smacks hand down on podium)) came to *any* of the businesses in my community and said anything

C2: ((angrily)) I think what we oughta do is put it next door to *your* house to see how *you* can live with it!

Audience: ((assorted chuckles in response to Citizen 2)). (Courtney, 2001)

"This" and "it" refer alternately to the day center for migrant workers and to the workers themselves. The issue, however, is not the center itself – that is, the housing structure – but the people slated to occupy it. There is anger and indignation in Citizen 1's manner of expression; he and members of his neighborhood association perceive that they have been slighted by the city. This is an understandable attitude, yet the implication is that the neighbors believe they have greater entitlement to a quality habitat than do the day laborers. Both Citizens 1 and 2 seem to put their own rights to desirable living space above those of the day laborers. The devaluation of these men is reinforced by a remark made by City Councilman Sam Allison, who said on camera that "what was a concern were the workers strewn up and down the street . . ." (Courtney, 2001). His use of the verb "strewn" to describe the placement of people seems a mismatch. One might think of litter being strewn. The application of this verb to human beings is tantamount to implying that they are disposable, or tantamount to human waste (see Fox, 1999).

Shaming for Linguistic Inferiority

Indeed, immigrants whose English is either very limited or in the process of emerging are the targets of more blaming and shaming than those who have already attained proficiency in English (Alba, 2004; Crawford, 2000). In some cases, based on stereotypes associated with phenotype, others' English language skills are cursorily evaluated to be sub- par.

Linguistic difference or incomplete mastery of the English language is considered an affront to some Americans. Diane, the Hoover Elementary School teacher who says she is disliked by her colleagues due to her blondeness, offers the following assessment of her students' families:

D: Well most of my kids are born in Los Angeles which means their parents have been here at least seven or eight years… how dare they live in this country and not learn English? I don't know why people are resistant to assimilation. I truly have no idea. . . I mean they wanna come here they want a better life it's obviously better than where they were. . . and I'm not saying don't keep your *cul*ture but it can be familiar but if you choose to come to America you have to give up something.

Diane's indignation ("how dare they?") represents an impotent ideological challenge. Shaming for not acquiring English is common practice, even though it is widely known that second language acquisition is a lengthy process composed of many stages and especially arduous for adults (Lightbown & Spada, 1999; Mitchell & Myles, 1998). Diane's remark calls up the perpetual argument as to whether assimilation or coexistent multiculturalism is preferable. Later in the film, she mentions her Russian grandparents' insistence on assimilating (incidentally, a fervent project of corporate America during the early 20th century (Feagin, 1997)). In Diane's worldview, those parents who after seven or eight years still cannot communicate in English should be ashamed of themselves:

D: When my grandparents came, they moved to New York, they came for a better life, they assimilated they gave their children American names, they learned English. My mother did not speak Russian; they learned English they wanted to be American. American. They were *proud* to be American. Now being American is a dirty word. (Simón, 1997)

This intimation reveals Diane's underlying motivation: to defend her American identity, to which language is most intimately bound. Diane presents her family as an exemplary model; referring back to one's personal history is a frequent tactic among established Americans who are opposed to native language retention or bilingualism (McGuire, 2004). Arcelia ("A"), another teacher-protagonist in *Fear and Learning at Hoover Elementary* whose family had migrated across the border to work the fields, had this family experience in adapting to American institutions:

A: I didn't just get up one day and say you know Mom and Dad I'm going to Stanford. And send me care packages and I'll be back during the holidays, thank you very much. That's not quite how it happened. My mother especially, but my father, as well, felt very uncomfortable, felt very angry and very very saddened by the choices I was making. How could I leave the family, how could I abandon them, were they not good enough for me now, would I someday be ashamed of them, because they couldn't read or write, or would I someday deny them, because they couldn't speak English. (Simón, 1997)

Arcelia describes the primacy of cohesion in her family's values, an important component of which is language. Her parents' fear that she might one day shun them represents the kind of familial pressure that children of immigrants today undoubtedly experience as well. This is an effect of cultural hybridization in the borderlands (Anzaldúa, 1999).

The following exchange between a man and a woman on the Lemon Grove School Board evinces the man's implicit disdain for "the Mexicans."

M: Well, I think they'd be very grateful for a school over in their own neighborhood. They live together, they work together, they have their own parties, they should have their own school.

W: Do you really think they'd want that?

M: My son tells me that Miss Markland has to repeat herself over and over again for those kids, it's embarrassing. For all the kids. (Espinosa, 1985)

His line of argumentation is that segregation is desirable to the Mexican students, for whom cultural cohesion is important. When the woman expresses doubt where he seems certain, he explains that the children's poor English language skills are a source of embarrassment for all. Thus, segregation is his proposed solution. The children's presumed inferiority is difficult to face and best be relocated, out of sight. A subsequent scene in the film is a gathering of Mexican parents at the home of one of the families, the language spoken is Spanish, with English subtitles provided:

M1: Look at what the gringos are doing now. They're always making our lives more difficult.

W1: ((emphatically gesturing)) But our children *must* go to school.

M1: It's not fair – the idea of using that barn for a school is crazy.

M2: Good evening. You all know why we're here tonight. We've all seen what they've built here on Olive Street. It's nothing more than a barn and they're calling it a school. Now we know *when* they plan on using it for our children. This is an *insult!* A *humiliation!*

M1: Why are they doing this to us now? I don't know why they want to treat our kids differently.

W1: This was all started by those ladies on Golden Avenue. They don't want *their* children mingling with Mexican children.

M2: And don't forget, *we* pay taxes too!

M3: Claro!

M2: We help support that school. ((emphasizing with right clenched fist raised, and left fist also clenched))

W1: Our children should attend school with the American kids. ((turning to face the lady next to her)) That's how Roberto learned to speak English.

W2: My children were born here. They're citizens.

M1: They're treating us like this just because we're Mexicans. (Espinosa, 1985)

    The second male interlocutor's comment that the new school is a barn, which was called "La Caballeriza" (Kellman, 1986), that is, a structure intended for animals – is an insult, demonstrates the injurious results of exclusionary power relations which facilitate exploitation in political and economic spheres and contribute to the reproduction of ideological power (Fairclough, 1989; Riggins, 1997). As Fairclough (1989) noted, "power is won, held and lost in social struggles" (p. 74). The parents put up a fight, and do so, successfully. While people with power in educational institutions often have no link to the capitalist class, they train children "to fit into and accept the existing system of class relations" (Fairclough, 1989, p. 33; see also Ollman, 2002). The woman's remark that their "children should attend school with the American kids," which is how her son learned to speak English, is supported by de la Garza and DeSipio's (1998) finding that Mexican Americans hold strong convictions that people residing in the U.S. should learn English.

    Finally, the remark that segregation is taking place "just because we're Mexicans" is accurate; as Ramirez (1988) noted, since traditional Mexican values are not as future-oriented or individualistic as those of the cultural majority, "it is no wonder that members of the dominant group are prejudiced against them"

(p. 139). This discussion leads into further consideration of discursive practice which the dominant cultural majority employs to distance itself from the immigrant Other.

Othering: Distancing the Immigrant

The third question posed by this study asks: What functions does Othering the borderlands immigrant effect and reify by (a) creating an us-versus-them dialectic? and (b) in rhetoric supporting militarization of the border?

The discursive act of Othering is an area which readily overlaps with blaming and shaming. Othering intentionally highlights the demarcation between 'us' and 'them' to maintain a dialectic (or, as Dockett and North-Schulte (2003) described, an attachment to difference) to support the social practice of blaming and shaming and to stigmatize the immigrant, which justifies the practice. In this section, the us-them dialectic is illuminated first as talk expressing ambivalence toward the immigrant Other and second as talk justifying physical exclusion. I then note how ambivalence, the simultaneous or alternating attraction and repulsion toward the Other, enables dehumanizing the Other by establishing psychological distance via the us-them mechanism. Finally, the us-them mindset leads to the expenditure of resources to keep the Other out by militarizing the international boundary.

Othering by Creating an Us-Them Dialectic

Much anti-immigrant talk functions to differentiate 'us' from 'them.' In this excerpt from Frontline's *Go Back to Mexico!*, the journalist/expositor Langewiesche introduces a disgruntled Mr. Fleming, who is offended by the poverty evident in the landscape inhabited by the Other:

F: There are whole portions of Los Angeles city. If you don't know where you're at, you'd swear you're in Tijuana! You cannot tell the difference. You cannot tell the difference. The barrio that exists in Tijuana and it looks exactly the same as the one in Los Angeles; as an American I'm offended by that! (Galán, 1994)

A prefatory explanation by Langewiesche informs viewers that, as a small business owner, Fleming is experiencing cultural anxiety as a result of being overwhelmed (and, it is inferred, threatened). An extension of this interpretation underscores Fleming's confusion. Twice he emphasizes that "you cannot tell the difference" between sections of Los Angeles and the barrio of the Mexican border city Tijuana. Here Fleming is disturbed by the fact that difference is blurred, and that the Other dare reshape the cultural landscape to reflect his own world. Fleming betrays a possible case of "Hispanophobia," which typically produces reactions of objections to street signs and other linguistic and material markers belonging to the Other (Crawford, 2000). This is the borderlands world inhabited by Anzaldúa's (1999) cultural hybrids.

The undeniable visibility of this very Other is expressed as fear by the headless voices in the vox pop sequence cited above on page 91:

"We've had two and a half years of hell! And there was about forty, fifty of them living out here; we, we, couldn't even step out our door at night" (Espinosa, 1989).

"Forty or fifty of them" is a significant threat to the speaker. It is no wonder that fear should polarize communities against them. As Jenna, the young mother residing in the Austin, Texas neighborhood to which a day laborer center is being relocated by the city, attempts to rationalize her opposition to this uncomfortable symbiosis with such an overwhelming quantity of Others:

J: I have a three-year-old that I worry a lot about and I wanna make sure that this neighborhood's a safe place to be (.) all the horror stories that I'd heard and seen from downtown (.) I did not want that in my neighborhood (.) and it wasn't a NIMBY situation I wasn't saying not in my backyard (.) what I was saying was that shouldn't be in anyone's backyard (.) it shouldn't be in a neighborhood at all! (Courtney, 2001)

First, Jenna asserts that she is speaking as a concerned mother, that she has good reason to feel protective and territorial. Jenna's reference to "all the horror stories I'd heard and seen from downtown" from her safe distance in the suburbs is not fully convincing. It can be assumed that the underlying concern is for her own happiness, and that of her neighbors. As Verkuyten (2003) explained, the notion of salvaging one group's happiness frequently functions as an argument for the exclusion of minority groups, or for the exclusion of that minority group's happiness. The speaker also denies the racist or ethnicist implications of her position when she advocates that "it" (i.e., the collectivity of immigrant laborers) does not belong "in anyone's backyard." In fact, the Other, dehumanized, doesn't deserve to "be in a neighborhood at all!" The insinuation is that some people are not fit to inhabit a respectable neighborhood for, if they do, they will sully her child. Though Jenna says where the workers do not belong (here, with us), she does not mention where they might belong. She simply wants them out of sight.

While the social problem of worker-Others infringing on a dominant group's territory originates in economic factors, the speakers (and filmmakers) never forthrightly acknowledge how the exploited labor of these low-cost immigrants sustains an international economic symbiosis in that the workers create huge profit margins for employers (Akers, 2004; Feagin, 1997).

Attachment to Difference
Think about this, we're fixing to double our population in about fifty years, okay, it's all due to immigration. About fifty years ninety percent of the population growth rate in this country will be due to immigrants and their descendants – not to people like you and me. (Courtney, 2001)

Whether expressed as overt or explicit racism, as in the above excerpt, or veiled and implicit, the attachment to difference is way of understanding how people feel justified in blaming and shaming the Other (Dockett & North-Schulte, 2003). Intolerance of difference in culture, worldview, priorities, appearance, and values catalyzes the anti-immigrant sensibility. In the clip below, the Other is framed as a menace to the politics of the nation- state, in part owing to race. The filmmakers cut back and forth between Harry and an anti-immigrant rally, where participants engage in a robust rendition of the *Star Spangled Banner*.

H: When do they become American? When they learn the meaning of democracy.

[Cut to rally]

Crowd: ((singing)) and the rockets' red glare!

[Cut back to Harry and Davida on lawn]

H: When they learn what this. . . What our country is all about.

[Cut back to rally]

Crowd: ((singing)) the bombs bursting in air

[Cut back to Harry and Davida on lawn]

H: this is something that these people I don't think will ever grasp.

[Cut back to rally]

Crowd: ((singing)) gave proof through the night, that our flag: was still there

[Cut back to Harry and Davida]

H: Caucasians. . are not going to benefit. (Lerner & Stirling, 1991)

At a rally of the *Coalition for Immigration Law Enforcement*, the chief rabble-rouser, Mr. O., presents a mandatory non-citizen identification card as a sign of progressive politics, advocating the polarization of us and them to drive public policy:
O: Thank you very much. It is a real pleasure to be here among

people who give a damn ((audience cheering and clapping)) Mr. [x x] set me up so well I am now on page five of my written notes ((audience laughing)) he proposed a card to identify the citizens and I think he has an excellent idea. Our borders would be a lot easier to protect if we had the card that told who the citizens were while the existing government did data banks that handled the details of making the decisions. So I am proposing a card of that nature. Now many people will say it won't work; it's not *pop*ular among people who resent change, people who don't want to think, but I do believe it can succeed among people such as yourself. *We* are Americans. *They* are not! (Lerner & Stirling, 1991)

As a reminder, Potter (2003) held that "...attitude expressions can be studied as talk designed for use in settings where there is a possibility of argument and where [an interlocutor] is simultaneously justifying a position and implicitly countering alternatives" (p. 74). Of great import to Mr. O. is national affiliation, and having that identity inscribed on paper. Such difference is considered sufficient justification for his proposal. (California State Senator Craven (R-Oceanside) introduced to the legislature a proposal that all people of Hispanic descent, being members of a "suspect class," carry such an ID card (Chavez, 1997, p. 62)). At the same time, the speaker anticipates criticism of his ideas: accusing the opposition of resenting change, of lesser resiliency than the anti-immigrant camp. This tack is regularly found in the videos of the American Patrol (Spencer, 2001) and the far right wing monthly publication *Middle American News*. (See also www.immigrationcontrol.com).

Ambivalence toward the Other is the recognition of difference which can manifest in creating psychological or physical distance. Conservative Latinos who, as naturalized American citizens, wish to dissociate themselves from recent immigrants of the same ethnic background or national heritage, often feel an underlying sense of ambivalence or divided allegiance. By adopting the attitudes of the dominant majority established immigrants tend to incline toward increasingly restrictive immigration policy to underscore their difference from new or would-be immigrants (Binder, Polinard, & Wrinkle, 1997; de la Garza & DeSipio, 1998). Carmen, a woman who works at a parent outreach center at Hoover Elementary School, reveals that she voted in favor of Proposition 187. The following excerpt represents the film's English subtitles for the original Spanish language text:

Carmen ((in Spanish)): This used to be a close community. It was very tranquil. People would take walks. We all knew each other. And now, you can't even take a walk. There are shootings. I've already been in two. And why? It's the people who have recently immigrated. They're not interested in cleanliness. They're not interested in union. They're not interested in helping one another. They just take services. Take services. Take services. But they give nothing. That's what I dislike about them. That's why I voted in favor of 187. That's why I tell you I'm a bad person. ((Laughs)) I don't know. Things have made me change so much. All those experiences I've had. I've changed ... a lot. And who knows what's ahead of me. (Simón, 1997)

Here Carmen embraces anti-immigrant rhetoric to justify her vote in favor of Proposition 187, speaking of "them" as unclean takers. Carmen laughs after she confides in the filmmaker that she is "a bad person," for she is aware that her gesture of alignment with the dominant majority represents a betrayal of her roots and of the community in which she lives and works. In creating psychological distance and framing the Other deictically, as Carmen does in clearly setting herself apart from "them," social actors give themselves permission to take an anti-immigrant stance.

Keeping the Other Out

The anti-immigrant project known as *Light Up the Border* appeared in two films, *Natives: Immigrant Bashing at the Border* (Lerner & Stirling, 1991) and *Go Back to Mexico!* (Galán, 1994). *New World Border* (Peek, 2001) also features actors in favor of building walls and enhancing border and human barrier controls. Two apparent effects of Border Patrol- implemented operations are to assuage the Other-fearing public that remedial federal action is being taken and to incite activism and protest among the public. Muriel Watson, spokesperson for *Light Up*, calmly explained to the camera:

M: *Light up the border* was a symbolic gesture (.) where Americans citizens who are concerned about the problems at the border came, parked in the road, turned on their headlights for about thirty minutes and then left (.) and then kept up the level of conversation about it (.) talked to the ah talk show hosts on the /ra:di:o: uh everybody was conversing about it\ the news media was attending to it (.) this was interpreted by some people as a uh anti-Mexican program (.) it had nothing to do (.) with that. (Lerner & Stirling, 1991)

Using sensationalistic or theatrical tactics to draw attention to an issue and foment social change can be seen as a manifestation of outlaw discourse, or supposing a logic that lies outside acceptable boundaries (Ono & Sloop, 2002). As Muriel explains, turning on the headlights was an activity to raise political awareness about the "uncontrolled flow of human beings coming across the international boundary into the United States" (Lerner & Stirling, 1991). The blunt denial of racism or nativism anticipates criticism; instead, in the speaker's worldview removing "the problems at the border" will ensure citizens' happiness (Verkuyten, 2003). Lighting up the border also exposes the Other's shame – and the stigma of being 'illegal.'

While Ms. Watson is serene in her delivery, Mr. Cavanaugh shows no restraint in relaying his fantasies about how to exclude – or eradicate – the Other:

C: on the other side of the border, if I were given the ability to do so, with unlimited reserves, it would be very simple. I would get the military down there, as we did in Saudi Arabia, put them across the border and anything that moves: has to be stopped and investigated. (Lerner & Stirling, 1991)

Such an explicitly negative expression of nationalism occurs in a context of confiding in the filmmaker. Harry, tending to his lawn in peace, similarly opines:

H: I would say get the army down there with machine guns…
((breaking into laugh)) and if you peppered these people with
machine guns they'd quit coming across, the military if you
would give them machine guns and give them authority to
shoot these people and if they shot a few of them and I mean
it's a, a, a really a cruel thing to say but if we have to stop them
this is the way to stop 'em. This is what Germany did to keep
people in their country and this is what we could do to keep
them from coming into our country. (Lerner & Stirling, 1991)

The oblique reference to the Berlin Wall romanticizes the
solutions to illicit border crossings associated with the Iron
Curtain era. The "negative symbolism of a border wall
between two friendly nations" (Dunn, 2003, pp. 201-202) and
the immediate analogy with the Berlin Wall provoked
"vociferous dissent" among those averse to Operation
Blockade in the El Paso, Texas area. The "wall-as-crime-
prevention" (Dunn, 2003, p. 206) strategy seemed too
extreme a reaction. In the above excerpt, Harry even
advocates violence in the name of preserving the boundaries
of the nation-state: The Other as an individual is of such little
value that s/he should be shot. Militarization at the Mexico-
U.S. border is visually contrasted with the Berlin Wall in *Go
Back to Mexico!* (Galán, 1994); shots of dismal scenes at the
Wall are voiced over by Langewiesche's narration:

L: Frankly, there are ways to seal a border. The Soviets showed
us how: it requires barbed wire watchtowers and guards and
some sort of more powerful deterrent. No one seriously
suggests that the United States use deadly force on its
perimeter, but those most concerned about illegal
immigration worry that arrest and deportation is no
punishment at all, that the southern border is just a revolving
door. (Galán, 1994)

Elsewhere the fantasy persists, but limits are acknowledged:
Man: we're not like East Germany, we can't have machine gun
towers and minefields. Now that's a way of stopping 'em but

America will never do that.

Muriel: no

Man: and if you have a moat then... then what that would do is that would cut down the police effort... is people are not just gonna swim through ten foot or twenty foot o' water maybe thirty foot forty foot wide... with a high wall you know a high wall on this side ((helicopter chopper noise))... if you're standing you can't wade in ten foot of water so if you swim-swim up to here, uh, you still have to get over an eight or a ten foot wall. (Lerner & Stirling, 1991)

Hard line military-style tactics is supported by public representatives as well, again, expressed in terms of a fascination with equipment or materials:

Congressman Duncan Hunter (from "Border Update – 1998"): The gentlemen who are building this fence are National Guardsmen . . . these folks are energetic they're enthusiastic they love what they're doing they know they're keeping drugs out of our country and they have high morale... we combed every single military base from Guam to Guantanamo and we found steel landing mat... a steel landing mat is approximately two feet wide ten feet long and it's a kinda steel that you use... to knit together to make a runway... like the ones we used in Desert Storm. . . that landing mat also makes a great fence. (Peek, 2001)

In 2005, the fantasy has begun to come true. Arizona's civilian Minutemen began patrolling the state's border with Mexico in attempt to take the law into their own hands (Kelly, 2005a & 2005b; see also the Minuteman Project Web site at: http://www.minutemanproject.com).

Counter-Discourse
The fourth question this study asks is: What counter-discursive strategies manifest alongside the extreme or mainstream debates on borderlands issues (a) in the form of

defense (or self-defense) of the migrant/immigrant and (b) in the form of protest as empowerment?

Counter-Discourse in Defense of the Migrant Worker

As defined in Chapter 2, outlaw discourse refers to rhetoric originating in marginalized communities which challenges the cultural truisms perpetuated in mainstream thinking by posing alternative worldviews (Ono & Sloop, 2002). I use the term counter discourse to allow for talk that may not possess the potential to foment social change or bring about the development of a culture of resistance, which is an aspect of outlaw discourse (hooks, 1991). Counter- and outlaw discourses belong to the bold, as well as to the innocent. *New World Border* (Peek, 2001) might be characterized as an overtly counter-discursive advocacy documentary in that it represents several social actors who authoritatively counter mainstream and anti-immigrant attitudes. The opening scene includes a poignant conversation between a young boy of seven or eight years old, Jacob ("J"), and his father ("F") while Jacob clings to the fence demarcating the international boundary between the U.S. and Mexico:

F: So what do you think about this fence here?

J: ((banging on fence)) I think it should be knocked down by a crane.

F: Why?

J: cuz it's stupid it makes my head burn.

F: yeah?

J: ((nods))

F: what do think about... what do you think about all the people that live on the other side of this fence?

J: I think they're nice

F: why do you think they have to build fences like this?

J: so there won't be across (but)… they should they should knock it down cuz, cuz, it's not fair for the… Mexican people back there . . cuz they did--they weren't doing anything.

F: yeah?

J: they just decided to… the Americans just decided to ((gestures widely, opening arms broadly to his side)) boom! close down th--close down this way. (Peek, 2001)

Little Jacob is not privy to the political machinations behind closing "down this way," but he feels that "it's not fair for the Mexican people back there … [because] they weren't doing anything" wrong. The child, at the locus of the aesthetically unappealing border fence, already recognizes that people are being excluded at the level of the nation-state and, recognizing the common humanity the Mexicans share with those on the American side, intuitively comes to their defense (Ono & Sloop, 2002). The innocent child's plaintive tone makes one wonder whether "they" *were* they doing anything wrong. Or, were they migrating as is the natural propensity among humans impelled to survive? Do geopolitical strictures thwart the human inclination to move? It is not within the scope of this study to address these questions. However, *New World Border*'s experts shed light on the global perspective by explaining the impact of NAFTA on influencing mass migration north from Mexico. As Armando Navarro, of *Impacto 2000*, implored the crowd assembled at the San Diego/Mexico fence which reaches all the way into the sea:

A: We must remember what this wall symbolizes! And it's a symbol of oppression, it's a symbol of exploitation, it's a division that has been created that's in contradiction to the spirit supposedly of NAFTA that is being created here in this country. (Peek, 2001)

The wall itself, like the Berlin Wall, represents an affront to human freedom. Fences and walls are, after all, used to define boundaries for animals or undesirable creatures (i.e., the stigmatized) who are meant to be oppressed and exploited. To revisit the animal theme briefly, several films depicted migrant laborers lashing out, in Spanish, with English subtitles. One elderly working immigrant spoke candidly of the inferior treatment received:

Man: We come in search of dollars, your precious commodity. With one of your dollars, we've earned enough for the whole day. You're so selfish. You treat us like *dogs*. That's what hurts us. (Espinosa, 1989)

In all of the ten films included in this analysis, only immigrants spoke of being treated like animals, a particularly debased way of characterizing the experience of being shamed. Later on the same man adds additional animals to the list when he speaks of impending eviction from the migrant squatter's camp is the central issue explored in *Uneasy Neighbors* (Espinosa, 1989):

Man: They'll soon kick us out of here. Where will we go? Will we continue shivering in the corners like coyotes, like dogs or lizards as I've said, and then what? ((shaking head)) no. (Espinosa, 1989)

An advocate of the people living in the camp, a reverend ("R") from a local church, speaks in their defense:

R: What many people don't realize is that these people are human beings and they have social needs like everybody else. They have social needs to be together to, to, share with each other their problems their moments of happiness and joy too. (Espinosa, 1989)

The reverend's claim that many people do not "realize that these people are human beings" is a striking statement. To the reverend, the notion of the supremacy of the nation-state transcending human rights is unconscionable (Bosniak, 1997). As he states elsewhere:

R: we just spent this winter two million dollars to save a couple of whales from being killed by the ice in the north pole and to tell me that we cannot house a few low-income people who work for us seems the greatest of absurdities. It's a matter of priorities; a matter of values in a society. Is it possible that we can value whales more than human beings? (Espinosa, 1989)

Bringing animals into the discourse, the reverend defends the oft-neglected humanity of the immigrant. In doing so he is shaming those who would shun the immigrant and his or her social and material necessities in favor of protecting animals, denying the commonalities among all human beings (Ono & Sloop, 2002). Another interlocutor stated that "[t]here are some Americans who appreciate us from their hearts, as fellow human beings. There are others who see us as animals. When they see us, they turn away" (Espinosa, 1989). The acknowledgment of being shamed and blamed often incites anger in the immigrant Other.

One angry immigrant interviewed at the Los Angeles County Hospital fumed, in Spanish (translated by English voiceover):

Man: I don't think they're stealing services. *What* service? Service means to offer improvement. No one leaves here better. They leave here tired of waiting. They leave here even sicker than when they came! It's time they stop blaming us. They keep saying that the state is broke because of us. No! The state is rich because of us, because *I* pay taxes, and I don't see those taxes; I don't benefit from them. (Galán, 1994)

This man speaks to the antagonistic relationship of the immigrant/minority to the dominant American cultural majority, which he implies takes advantage of immigrants by keeping them marginalized. Though they pay income tax, they remain on the perimeter of societal inclusion, always members of an outgroup (JanMohamed & Lloyd, 1990).

Protest as Empowerment

Migrants who cross the border are often of strong constitution, empowered by their convictions, such as Ramón, a chief protagonist of *Los Trabajadores=The Workers*. His personal protest in the following excerpt, dubbed over in English, is evident:

Ramón ((subtitled from Spanish)): What I did was to come here illegally and this is against the law of the United States. But it is not against the law of my family, nor is it against my law. Even if they're American, they can't tell me "you can't work to support your family," no. This is the right that I have, to make sure my family is okay, and no one can take that away from me. It's the right I've earned, it's mine, it's my responsibility. My daughters are growing up and they really need me down there, but the economic situation doesn't permit this. We need to be strong and see the reality of life. There's no way you can compare a life in a place where you live with your family, with a life where you live alone. If you tell me to choose, I'll choose Mexico always. (Courtney, 2001)

Ramón is determined to defy the law. His values are in stark opposition to those of conservatives who value obedience to the law for its own sake, regardless of its repercussions for significant Other sectors of humanity. Ramón identifies his responsibility to family as transcending borders; his choice to work undocumented in the United States consciously challenges cultural truisms prevalent in mainstream thinking and works as an alternative worldview which could potentially influence others in similar marginalized positions (hooks, 1991; Ono & Sloop, 2002).

Among borderlands artists an exemplary outlaw voice belongs to Guillermo Gómez-Peña, whose subversive performance piece *Border Brujo* (1991), is an ironic meditation on immigrant stereotypes. The performance implicitly conveys negative attitudes via ironic humor (Blommaert & Verschueren, 1998). As Riggins (1997) noted, minority discourses tend to be "contradictory, complex, and ironic" (p. 6) and, in spite of their defiance reveal "lingering elements of shame and self-hatred [as] a result of exposure to the dominant culture's educational institutions and to psychological masochism" (p. 7). The following excerpt from Gómez-Peña's work demonstrates the impact of the dominant group's ambivalence toward the minority group:

G.-P.: ((rhythmically and slowly moving fist/forearm forward and backward, his right fist, adorned with long teeth)) Iya speaka Spanish, therefore you hate me; Iya speak in English, therefore they hate me; Iya speaka Spanglish therefore shea speaks Engleñon; I speak in tongues therefore you desire me ((gets into babbling in tongues)); Iya speak to you therefore you kill me; Iya speak therefore you change; Iya speak in English therefore I hate you; pero cuandar español, but when I speaka Spanish I adore you; why carajos do I ah speaka Spanish; political praxis carmal I mean. (Gómez-Peña & Artenstein, 1991)

No matter what language the Other speaks, s/he is hated and, at the same time, desired. The ingroup's attachment to Otherness necessitates an opposite, and language clearly marks that opposition. In the next excerpt, Gómez-Peña conjures up the animal metaphor vis-à-vis English-speaking ability, as if substandard English proficiency can be equated with being subhuman:

G.-P.: please, please! Forgive my bad English . . . I came too old to this country and I haven't been domesticated yet. (Gómez-Peña & Artenstein, 1991)

In the following excerpt, Gómez-Peña dredges up a familiar string of stereotypes, evoking his physically apparent Otherness and, while hinting at the tangible threat that that represents, turning the tables (Stangor & Crandall, 2000):
G.-P.: please, *please*! Don't touch me. I've got typhoid and malaria (.) don't you dare touch me! I haven't been docu*men*ted yet! My back is wet, my nipples are hard. I'm ready to fight... I'm ready to rave. Don't like me too much, 'cause I'm a drug

smuggling welfare recipient to be, sexist communist [x x x x x] devoted to the overthrow of the US government and the art world. Oh just kidding. *Don't like me too much.* I'm just a deterritorialized chilango who claims to be a Chi*cano*, and I'm not even eligible for amnesty because I never, *never* documented my work. The only photos of my performances are in the archives of the FBI and I'm a bit too shy to ask them for copies. Can anyone document me *please*! *Can anyone take a photo of this memorable occasion! Come on!* For the archives on border culture! For the history of performance art! Can anyone be so kind as to authenticate my existence! Hmmmm I'm not authentic enough! (Gómez- Peña & Artenstein, 1991)

Here Gómez-Peña gloats over his status as Other, pleading with his projected audience for salvation. His chiding that he is "not authentic enough" taunts the system for insisting on official documentation as a means of attaining fully human status. Authorized and authentic become interchangeable, synonymous.

Gómez-Peña's work relies on self-deprecation, humor, irony, and allusions to the mysterious, fearsome, and transitional void occupied by all cultural hybrids in the borderlands to suggest an alternative reality, to vividly call attention to the identity crisis experienced by the migrant straddling the fence. As Anzaldúa (1999) wrote, border culture is the result of "two worlds merging to form a third country" (p. 25). The anti-immigrant discourse expresses opposition to this inevitable emergence of new cultural forms and the resultant changing physical landscape. Anti-immigrant activists remain attached to the difference between 'us' and 'them,' yet are often ambivalent because of an undeniable symbiosis which is seldom acknowledged. While attempts to keep the Other out may be in vain, the anti-immigrant and counter-discourses continue to compete, supporting the social practices and policies which determine 'reality.'

CHAPTER 5

Conclusions

This study represents a discursive psychological analysis of a chronic social issue of great complexity, immigration issues in the Mexico-U.S. borderlands. I have examined this issue from a discursive psychological perspective, wherein talk represents an entrée into the map of individuals' psychological landscapes vis-à-vis articulations of perceptions of the outlying world. In analyzing the utterances of social actors, this work embraces the view that the nature of talk is socially constructed. By the same token, the nature of human experience is subjectively constructed (de Silva, 1979; Olendzki, 2003). Speakers draw on various discursive or rhetorical resources to justify their own 'truth' and to attempt to invalidate or ignore the truths of their opponents. Those whose knowledge of a subject is nil or limited will nevertheless express opinions using language "which then constructs the reality that is thereafter perceived" (Falk, 2001, p. 22). In turn, the rhetoric continues to reify the reality that it constructs (Wetherell & Potter, 1992). In studying talk from a discursive or rhetorical perspective, analysts' aim is to "see how the themes of ideology are instantiated in ordinary talk, and how speakers are part of, and continuing, the ideological history of the discursive themes which they are using" (Billig, 2001, p. 218).

As Bakhtin (1981) argued in his dialogic case for linguistic reality, 'true' meaning is negotiated in relation to temporally, sequentially, and historically situated utterances. Fairclough (1989, 1999, 2001) conceived of this situatedness in terms of intertextuality; that is, thematically related texts are interconnected and tend to reveal an internally consistent body of representations. Foucault conceived of truth simply as error which over time had hardened into reality (as cited in Hartstock, 1990). It is in this sense that the ten films selected for this study reveal ideological cohesion. The semantic categories by which the discourse extracts were discussed (see Table 2, Chapter 3, and Figure 1) demonstrate that the themes and markers that regularly surfaced in the films support the hypotheses of Lee, Ottati, and Hussain (2001) and Short and Magaña (2002). The chief justifications and arguments provided for anti-immigrant sentiment are: (1) nativism; (2) concern for the national economy; and (3) issues of legality or the importance of obedience to law. I conclude that anti-immigrant talk as captured in these filmic representations contributes to reinforcing the stereotypes, folk beliefs, and commonsense ideologies that circulate to maintain conservative ideals of cultural assimilation, advocacy of English-Only policies and, ultimately, exclusion from the U.S. based on ethnicity or national origin (Blommaert & Verschueren, 1998; Riggins, 1997).

Broader conclusions resulting from this analysis include: (1) issues of immigration present an ideological dilemma, with no perfect solution; (2) a primary concern of anti-immigrant activists is preserving their own sense of happiness to the exclusion of Others' happiness; and (3) attachment to difference is an underlying motivation for prejudice against immigrant-Others.

The Ideological Dilemma of 'the Immigration Problem'

The 'immigration problem' poses an "ideological dilemma." Symbiosis among diverse cultures is inevitable in the U.S. (Billig, 1988), particularly in the borderlands, though the borderlands are rapidly expanding into southern states which previously attracted few Mexican and Latin American immigrants. On the one hand, there exists tolerance of diversity, multiculturalism, or cultural pluralism; on the other hand, intolerance of the Other at best amounts to advocacy of assimilation. While nativists have traditionally been in favor of curtailing immigration, which currently appears to be the trend, 'Americanization' or anglicization was always the goal with regard to immigrants already authorized to reside in the U.S. This agenda has been widely embraced by U.S. capitalists who thrive on the labor of newly arrived immigrants. As Feagin (1997) observed, "every time that nativists have succeeded in getting restrictive legislation, business interests needing cheap labor have found ways around the laws" (p. 18). In recent years restrictive legislative measures have included California's Proposition 187 and Arizona's Proposition 200 while recently the administration of President George W. Bush plans to revive a contemporary bracero[7] program.

A large part of the problem is that the mainstream media and politicians generally avoid lucid explication of the relationship of global corporate interests to the loss of adequate employment for U.S. working classes whose livelihoods are indeed threatened by competitive immigrant labor. Few of the films I examine elucidate viewers as to the integral role of corporate America in exacerbating 'the immigrant problem.' One exception is Casey Peek's *New World Border* (2001), which discusses the effect of NAFTA on the Mexican agricultural industry. Another film which outlines the corporate connection, but which was not included in this study, is Ursula Biemann's *Performing the Border*, which deals with the serial murders of women in the border town of Ciudad Juarez, Mexico, where many multinational corporations have established plants in order to exploit their cheap labor.

Filmmakers' rhetorical strategies often mirror those of politicians who fail to disclose the intricacies of economic forces involved, and allow immigrants to continue in their roles as scapegoats (Short & Magaña, 2002). Rather than expose the increasing hegemony of capitalistic culture as the grand driving force behind the multiple problems created by 'illegal' immigration, filmmakers compulsorily make emotional appeals to the audience with tales of immigrants' personal hardship, as if sympathy will lead to social action sufficient to remedy the dilemmas. Portraying immigrants as victims of political and discursive battles may do immigrants

---

[7] A Mexican laborer permitted to enter the United States and work for a limited period of time, especially in agriculture.

a disservice. As the data show, not all immigrants are passive or powerless. In any event, "power is not monolithic," nor do two distinct groups of people occupy absolute camps for "the powerful and the powerless" (Cameron et al., 1999), p. 153). Typically, powerful immigrants are underrepresented in favor of sentimental vignettes evoking cliché images of the virtuous immigrant in the eighteenth century tradition of romanticizing the tender Noble Savage (Berkhofer, 1978). Or, powerful immigrants are depicted as threats. The extreme viewpoints that characterize depictions of what amounts to intercultural conflict underline the debate's absurdity in avoiding the middle path, because "both ends of the political spectrum base their arguments on populist and emotional appeals" (Magaña, 2003, p. 4).

Bipolar Extremes in the Discourse

Extremism is a primary feature of both anti-immigrant discourse as well as pro- immigrant discourse. At one extreme, the films produced by the right-wing American Patrol (aka Voices of Citizens Together) express a fear of Mexican reclamation of lands which they dub "Mexifornia" or "Amexica" (Spencer, 2001). The rhetoric in these films preys upon the ignorance of the average citizen, "creating doomsday 'Third World-ization' scenarios out of a jumble of unrelated facts and unsubstantiated assertions" (Feagin, 1997, p. 31). Extremism leads interlocutors to advocate violence, even murder, in the name of keeping the Other out (Lerner & Stirling, 1991). More frequently, vigilantes patrolling crossing routes may refuse to assist immigrants sick from dehydration by denying them water or refusing to facilitate access to emergency medical care (Annerino, 1999). Further, though not an aim of this work, it was generally noted that anti anti-immigrant ideologies tended to portray immigration 'restrictionists' in the worst possible light, and vice versa, when in fact such attitudes lie along a continuum in which there are many gradations.

Happiness and Attitudes toward Immigration

An underlying motivation for an anti-immigrant agenda often came down to the simple matter of happiness, since immigrants are routinely blamed for interfering with conditions that might otherwise secure happiness for the status quo. As Verkuyten (2003) observed, "... unhappiness implies a need for or a right to change, whereas happiness is an argument for the status quo, and even domination. ... Happiness is a basic individual right" (p. 152).

Whereas an anti-immigrant interlocutor or nativist may be motivated by a concern for his or her individual happiness, which entails arguments justifying the exclusion of migrant border crossers, to an immigrant or liberal immigrant advocate happiness might entail humanitarian arguments in favor of inclusion. From the perspective of socially engaged Buddhist philosophy, "... happiness cannot be attained alone. The most satisfying and lasting happiness involves a life not only free of hatred and fear, but lived in compassion and action for others" (Chappell, 2003, p. 259).

Attachment to Difference

Blaming and shaming the immigrant for social problems offers clear evidence for a psychological attachment to difference, a concept central to Buddhist psychology (Dockett & North-Schulte, 2003; Nhât Hanh, 2003). Difference manifests outwardly in cultural and social institutions, values and practices. The assignment of stigma, which encourages exclusion, derives from a fundamental attachment to difference; it is a means of differentiating oneself and one's group affiliation from 'less desirable' others. Yet attachment to difference leads social actors to discursively dehumanize immigrants by equating them with animals, or waste, or appraising them solely in terms of their economic impact. Attempts to prove the superiority of one group over another merely brings about more suffering and negates the possibility of joy and contentment among all beings (Dockett & North-Schulte, 2003).

The ideological dilemmas posed by immigration issues are typically discussed in terms of legal or economic concerns, but can actually be approached in a radically different manner. If it is accepted that reality is a subjective construction, shaped by the circulation and reproduction of discourse, it is possible to consciously reconstruct one's worldview by acknowledging the wisdom of a basic tenet of Buddhist social activism: All beings are independent, and the happiness of each person depends on the happiness of all.

What I am proposing as one of very few tenable solutions to a dilemmatic situation is social transformation that begins with individuals taking personal responsibility for the transformation of their attitudes. This means finding compassion for those who obstinately refuse to compromise by working with their 'opponents,' and moving away from obdurate extremist positions. If social peace and happiness are to be achieved, then social responsibility for the well-being of all beings must be shared. Individuals should recognize and collaborate with a diversity of people and opinions, and develop an attitude of openness in order to understand Others' perspectives (Chappell, 2003).

The adoption of a Buddhist psychological ontology or philosophy presents a strong possibility for the amelioration of suffering caused by the estrangement created by the social practices of blaming, shaming, and Othering. To reiterate the insight of Thich Nhât Hanh (2003), suffering and unhappiness "escalate when we are overcome with anger and try to punish and inflict suffering on the other side" (p. 91). Individuals become addicted to their outrage and anger (Thurman, 2005). In blaming and inflicting more suffering on the other side by way of punitive actions, the only result is a never-ending chain of more unhappiness. (So while one's own happiness might motivate anti-immigrant actions, such actions contribute to the perpetuation of unhappiness in the social milieu.) As Olendzki (2003) explained, the study of reality is actually the study of how humans construct their experience of the world. By moving toward a conscious construction, people have the ability to create happiness and peaceful symbiosis.

Pedagogical Implications
The pedagogical implications of this work are manifold. In

terms of ESL education, the subject matter is compelling in two main ways: from a sociolinguistic perspective on language teaching, and as suitable material for content-based instruction (CBI).

First, it is important to teach context-appropriate language use or pragmatic information to ESL students. International or immigrant students may have had only limited or no exposure to historically significant or contemporary social issues and concepts pertaining to the plethora of ethnic groups in the U.S. As a result, they may be unfamiliar with prevailing attitudes and stereotypes, as well as nuances, connotations, or potentially pejorative meanings associated with specific vocabulary or phraseology relative to immigrant or marginalized cultural groups. For purposes of social survival, it would be vital to teach the ramifications of employing terms such as "illegal" or "alien," and various other racial epithets and slurs. Often newcomers lack the skill to gauge the gravity of utilizing certain sensitive language in specific contexts.

Second, the subject of immigration is ideal for the development of a content-based curriculum for use by adult school, college, or university level students at the upper intermediate or advanced level (see Snow & Brinton, 1997). The theme of immigration offers a wide range of stimulating and controversial topics for exploration, and should be of great relevance to and hence sustain the interest and motivation of students who choose to live and study abroad in the U.S. A primary textbook and videotape companion could provide the material for selected use over a semester or provide a yearlong curriculum in an integrated skills course. In devising a textbook or curriculum proposal, Stoller and Grabe's (1997) Six-T's Approach (comprised of Themes, Texts, Topics, Threads, Tasks, and Transitions) provides a solid foundational structure.

Tentative topics include the specific histories of immigrant groups to the United States, such as Chinese heading to build the railroads or find their fortunes during the Gold Rush,

Laotian refugees flocking to the coast of California following the Vietnam War, or Cubans or Haitians attempting the oft-precarious boat trip to the Florida coast. Attitudes toward immigrants and immigration and the history of nativism along with the dubious 'melting pot' concept (imported from England in 1908) could also be tapped into with a variety of related interpretive or affective tasks. Oral skills could be developed vis-à-vis debates on controversial, philosophical topics such as the pros and cons of assimilation versus multiculturalism or tolerance of diversity. For further conversation as well as writing practice, students could be probed to reflect on their culture's or country's particular truisms or 'commonsense' norms and values, and to write about these in relation to their developing experiential knowledge of the U.S. or of their peers' countries. They might also reflect on immigration issues in their home countries, such as Koreans residing in Japan, Muslims in various European countries, and Turks in Germany. The possibilities are multiple.

Finally, the films themselves (see Table 1, Chapter 3) are excellent texts for integration into a CBI classroom setting, particularly that which focuses on the interrelationships among social, political, and economic issues. Adequate activities in advance of and following screenings would need to be developed to maximize the films' pedagogical potential.

Limitations and Future Research

This study is limited in that it relies on extant data already 'cut' by film editors. However, such editing was not problematic for the purposes of this work, which is concerned with the discourse available to the public as representative of ideological notions serving to reinforce social attitudes through replication. One dimension that might have been explored was presenting film excerpts to research participants and interviewing them to obtain their reactions to the various issues and attitudes under controversy, with particular focus on the attitudes perceived to be inherent in discursive modes of expression and semantics.

Additionally, in order to maintain a manageable scope for this study, just ten nonfiction films were carefully selected for the final phase of analysis from an original pool of over 30 films. Some films from the larger borderlands cinema oeuvre were not included because, while they certainly dealt with relevant social issues in the borderlands, they may have focused too narrowly on the personal narratives or meditations of singled-out actors and included little interaction between or among interlocutors. Or, some of the films relied too heavily on expository "voice of God" narration, emphasizing the filmmaker's point of view over that of actors (Nichols, 1991).

Possibilities for future research on anti-immigrant attitudes and how these weave their way into mainstream discourse to blame, shame, and otherwise 'scapegoat' the immigrant are myriad. Although this study was restricted to discourse isolated from complex filmic texts, it could be reworked from a semiotic approach. That is, one might examine the interaction of text, image, and symbol to create and convey meaning and rhetoric, in the tradition of Barthes (1977) and other semioticians too numerous to mention here.

Further, the theme of attitudes toward immigrants, immigration, and the problematic construct of the nation-state merit close examination within the context of the social scientific research interview. As put forth in a thought-provoking collection of articles edited by van den Berg, Wetherell, and Houtkoop-Steenstra (2003), the social research interview can be analyzed as a co-constructed form of social practice in which class, race, and social relations are reproduced and reified. The research interview itself invariably involves rhetorical power struggles identical to those inherent in many discursive interactions involving interlocutors of unequal power relations.

Finally, no study of merit is ever complete. There are always more angles from which to explore and explain any given social phenomenon. It is my fervent hope that this work adequately contributes to the growing body of inquiries into attitudes toward immigrants in the U.S., and that it inspires introspection and compassion among all who take the time to read it.

REFERENCES

Akers, J. (2004). U.S. Border Patrol strategies are cruel and ineffective. In M. E. Williams (Ed.), *Immigration: Opposing viewpoints* (pp. 126-134). Farmington Hills, MI: Greenhaven Press.

Alba, R. (2004). *Language assimilation today: Bilingualism persists more than in the past, but English still dominates.* Retrieved January 6, 2005, from University at Albany, Lewis Mumford Center for Comparative Urban and Regional Research Web site: http://mumford.albany.edu/children/reports/languag e_assimilation/ language_assimilation01.htm

Aleinkoff, T. A. (2000). Illegal employers. *American Prospect, 11*(25), 15-17.

Alicke, M. D. (2000). Culpable control and the psychology of blame. *Psychological Bulletin, 126*(4), 556-574.

Alonso-Zaldivar, R. (2004, October 31). They won't touch this hot potato. *Los Angeles Times*, pp. A1, A27.

Alonso-Zaldivar, R. (2005, March 30). U.S. to bolster Arizona border security. *Los Angeles Times*, p. A12.

Annerino, J. (1999). *Dead in their tracks: Crossing America's desert borderlands.* New York: Four Walls Eight Windows.

Anzaldúa, G. (1999). *Borderlands / La frontera: The new mestiza.* (2nd ed.). San Francisco: Aunt Lute Books.

Auster, L. (2004). Immigration is harming American culture. In M. E. Williams (Ed.), *Immigration: Opposing viewpoints* (pp. 71-79). Farmington Hills, MI: Greenhaven Press.

Austin, J. L. (1999). How to do things with words. In A. Jaworski & N. Coupland (Eds.), *The discourse reader* (pp. 63-75). London: Routledge.

Bakhtin, M. M. (1981). *The dialogic imagination: Four essays.* M. Holquist (Ed.). & C. Emerson & M. Holquist (Trans.). Austin: University of Texas Press.

Barnes, B., Palmary, I., & Durrheim, K. (2001). The denial of racism: The role of humor, personal experience, and self-censorship. *Journal of Language and Social Psychology, 20*(3), 321-338.

Barthes, R. (1977). *Image, music, text.* New York: Hill and Wang.

Berg, C. R. (1992). Bordertown, the assimilation narrative, and the Chicano social problem film. In C. A. Noriega (Ed.), *Chicanos and film: Representation and resistance* (pp. 29- 46). Minneapolis: University of Minnesota Press.

Berkhofer, Jr., R. F. (1978). *The white man's Indian: Images of the American Indian from Columbus to the present.* New York: Vintage Books.

Biberman, H. J. (Director), Jarrico, P. (Producer), & Wilson, M. (Writer). (1954). *Salt of the earth* [Motion picture]. United States: Independent Productions Corporation and the International Union of Mine, Mill, and Smelter Workers.

Biemann, U. (Producer). (1999). *Performing the border* [Motion Picture]. United States: Women Make Movies.

Biernat, M., & Dovidio, J. F. (2000). Threat and the social construction of stigma. In T. F. Heatherton, R. E. Kleck, M. R. Hebl, & J. G. Hebl (Eds.), *The social psychology of stigma* (pp. 88-125). New York and London: The Guilford Press.

Billig, M. (2001). Discursive, rhetorical, and ideological messages. In M. Wetherell, S. Taylor, & S. J. Yates (Eds.), *Discourse theory and practice: A reader* (pp. 210-221). London: Sage.

Billig, M., Condor, S., Edwards, D., Gane, M., Middleton, D., & Ridley, A. (1988). *Ideological dilemmas: A social psychology of everyday thinking.* London & Newbury Park, CA: Sage.

Binder, N. E., Polinard, J. L., & Wrinkle, R. D. (1997). Mexican American and Anglo attitudes toward immigration reform: A view from the border. *Social Science Quarterly, 78*(2), 324-337.

Blommaert, J. & Verschueren, J. (1998). *Debating diversity: Analysing the discourse of tolerance.* New York: Routledge.

Brothers, J. (2005, February 27). Shame may not be so bad after all. *Parade: The Sunday Newspaper Magazine,* pp. 4-5.

Bruner, J. (1985). *Actual worlds, possible worlds.* Cambridge, Massachusetts: Harvard University Press.

Calvo, L. (2002). "Lemme stay, I want to watch": Ambivalence in borderlands cinema. In M. Habell-Pallán &

M. Romero (Eds.), *Latino/a popular culture* (pp. 73-81). New York: New York University Press.

Cameron, D., Frazer, E., Harvey, P., Rampton, B., & Richardson, K. (1999). Power/knowledge: The politics of social science. In A. Jaworski & N. Coupland (Eds.), *The discourse reader* (pp. 141-157). New York: Routledge.

Carbó, T. (1997). Who are they? The rhetoric of institutional policies toward the indigenous populations of postrevolutionary Mexico. In S. H. Riggins (Ed.), *The language and politics of exclusion: Others in discourse* (pp. 88-108). Thousand Oaks, CA: Sage.

Chang, R. (1997). A meditation on borders. In J. F. Perea (Ed.), *Immigrants out!: The new nativism and the anti-immigrant impulse in the United States*. New York and London: New York University Press.

Chappell, D. W. (2003). Buddhist social principles. In K. H. Dockett, G. R. Dudley-Grant & C. P. Bankart (Eds.)., *Psychology and Buddhism: From individual to global community* (pp. 259-274). New York: Kluwer Academic / Plenum Publishers.

Charmaz, K. (2004). Grounded theory. In S. N. Hesse-Biber, & P. Leavy (Eds.), *Approaches to qualitative research: A reader on theory and practice* (pp. 496-521). New York: Oxford University Press.

Collier, Jr., J. C., & Collier, M. (1986). *Visual anthropology: Photography as research method*. Albuquerque: University of New Mexico Press.

Courtney, H. (Producer/Director/Editor). (2001). *Los trabajadores=the workers* [Motion picture]. United States: New Day Films.

Crandall, C. S. (2000). Ideology and lay theories of stigma: The justification of stigmatization. In T. F. Heatherton, R. E. Kleck, M. R. Hebl, & J. G. Hebl (Eds.), *The social psychology of stigma* (pp. 126-150). New York and London: The Guilford Press.

Crawford, J. (2000). *At war with diversity: U.S. language policy in an age of anxiety*. Clevedon, England: Multilingual Matters.

D'Souza, D. (2002). *Letters to a young conservative*. New York: Basic Books.

Davis, M. (2002). Foreword. In J. Nevins, *Operation gatekeeper:*

The rise of the "illegal alien" and the making of the U.S.-Mexico boundary. New York and London: Routledge.

de la Garza, R. O., & DeSipio, L. (1998). Interests not passions: Mexican-American attitudes toward Mexico, immigration from Mexico, and other issues shaping U.S.-Mexico relations. *International Migration Review, 32*(2), 401-422.

de Silva, M. W. P. (1979). *An introduction to Buddhist psychology.* New York: Barnes & Noble Books.

Dockett, K. H. & North-Schulte, D. (2003). Transcending self and other: Mahayana principles of integration. In K. H. Dockett, G. R. Dudley-Grant & C. P. Bankart (Eds.), *Psychology and Buddhism: From individual to global community* (pp. 215-238). New York: Kluwer Academic / Plenum Publishers.

Dovidio, J. F., Major, B., & Crocker, J. (2000). Stigma: Introduction and overview. In T. F. Heatherton, R. E. Kleck, M. R. Hebl, & J. G. Hebl (Eds.), *The social psychology of stigma* (pp. 1-28). New York and London: The Guilford Press.

Duncan, M. M. (2004) National origins quotas should be retained. In M. E. Williams (Ed.), *Immigration: Opposing viewpoints* (pp. 59-67). Farmington Hills, MI: Greenhaven Press.

Dunn, T. (2003). The border wall campaign: Democratic debate versus bureaucratic authority. In P. Vila (Ed.), *Ethnography at the border* (pp. 199-235). Minneapolis: University of Minnesota Press.

Edwards, D. (2003). Analyzing racial discourse: The discursive psychology of mind-world relationships. In H. van den Berg, M. Wetherell, and H. Houtkoop-Steenstra (Eds.), *Analyzing race talk: Multidisciplinary approaches to the interview* (pp. 31-48). Cambridge: Cambridge University Press.

Espinosa, P. (Producer/Writer/Director). (1989). *Uneasy neighbors* [Motion picture]. United States: KPBS-TV.

Espinosa, P. (Producer/Writer). (1985). *The Lemon Grove incident* [Motion picture]. United States: KPBS-TV.

Fairclough, N. (1989). *Language and power.* London and New York: Longman.

Fairclough, N. (1999). Linguistic and intertextual analysis within discourse. In A. Jaworski & N. Coupland (Eds.), *The discourse reader* (pp. 183-211). London: Routledge.

Fairclough, N. (2001). Critical discourse analysis as a method in social scientific research. In R. Wodak & M. Meyer (Eds.), *Methods of critical discourse analysis* (pp. 121-138). London and Thousand Oaks, CA: Sage.

Falk, G. (2001). *Stigma: How we treat outsiders.* Amherst, NY: Prometheus Books.

Feagin, J. R. (1997). Old poison in new bottles. In J. F. Perea, (Ed.). (1997). *Immigrants out!: The new nativism and the anti-immigrant impulse in the United States* (pp. 13- 43). New York and London: New York University Press.

Fox, C. F. (1999). *The fence and the river: Culture and politics at the U.S.-Mexico border.* Minneapolis: University of Minnesota Press.

Galán, H. (Producer/Director). (1994). *Frontline: Go back to Mexico!* [Motion picture]. United States: PBS.

Gardner, H. (1983). *Frames of mind.* New York: Basic Books.

Geertz, C. (1980). Blurred genres: The refiguration of social thought. *The American Scholar, 49*(2), 165-179.

Geertz, C. (1984). Distinguished lecture: Anti anti-relativism. *American Anthropologist, 86*(2), 263-278.

Glaser, B. G. & Strauss, A. L. (1967). *The discovery of grounded theory.* Chicago: Aldine Publishing Company.

Gómez-Peña, G. (Writer/Performer), & Artenstein, I. (Producer/Director). (1991). *Border brujo* [Motion picture]. United States: Third World Newsreel.

Gómez-Peña, G. (1994). The free art agreement/El tratado de libre cultura. In C. Becker (Ed.), *The subversive imagination: Artists, society, and social responsibility* (pp. 208- 222). New York and London: Routledge.

Goodman, N. (1978). *Ways of worldmaking.* Indianapolis, IN: Hackett Publishing Company.

Gorman, A. (2005, May 5). Volunteers to patrol border near San Diego. *Los Angeles Times,* pp. B1, B10.

Guimond, S., Begin, G., & Palmer, D. L. (1989). Education and causal attributions: The development of "person-blame" and "system-blame" ideology. *Social Psychology Quarterly, 52*(2), 126-140.

Gutiérrez, D. G. (1995). *Walls and mirrors: Mexican Americans, Mexican immigrants, and the politics of ethnicity.* Berkeley and Los

Angeles: University of California Press.

Hartstock, N. (1990). Rethinking modernism: Minority vs. majority theories. In A. R. JanMohamed & D. Lloyd (Eds.), *The nature and context of minority discourse* (pp. 17- 36). Oxford and New York: Oxford University Press.

Heatherton, T. F., Kleck, R. E., Hebl, M. R., & Hebl, J. G. (2000). (Eds.), *The social psychology of stigma*. New York and London: The Guilford Press.

Henwood, K. & Pidgeon, N. (2003). Grounded theory in psychological research. In P. M. Camic, J. E. Rhodes, & L. Yardley (Eds.), *Qualitative research in psychology: Expanding perspectives in methodology and design* (pp. 131-155). Washington, D.C.: American Psychological Association.

hooks, b. (1994). *Outlaw culture: Resisting representations*. New York and London: Routledge.

JanMohamed, A. R., & Lloyd, D. (1990). Introduction: Toward a theory of minority discourse: What is to be done? In A. R. JanMohamed & D. Lloyd (Eds.), *The nature and context of minority discourse* (pp. 1-16). Oxford and New York: Oxford University Press.

Kellman, S. G. (1986, September 5). Lemon Grove: Remembrance of a sour past. *The San Antonio Light*. Retrieved March 11, 2005 from http://electriciti.com/-espinosa/productions/lemonsal.htm

Kelly, D. (2004, June 20). A hospital on border going over edge. *Los Angeles Times*, p. A17. Kelly, D. (2005a, April 2). Minutemen prepare to lay down the law. *Los Angeles Times*, p. A15.

Kelly, D. (2005b, April 25). Illegal immigration fears have spread. *Los Angeles Times*, pp. A1 & A14.

Kuhn, T. S. (1996). *The structure of scientific revolutions.* (3rd ed.) Chicago: University of Chicago Press.

Lamb, S. (1996). *The trouble with blame: Victims, perpetrators, and responsibility*. Cambridge, MA: Harvard University Press.

Lee, Y.-T., and Ottati, V. (2002). Attitudes toward immigration policy: The roles of in- group—out-group bias, economic concern, and obedience to law. *The Journal of Social Psychology, 142*(5), 617-634.

Lee, Y.-T., Ottati, V., and Hussain, I. (2001). Attitudes toward "illegal" immigration into the United States: California Proposition 187. *Hispanic Journal of Behavioral Sciences, 23*(4), 430-443.

Lerner, J., Stirling, S., & the University of Southern California (Producers). (1991). *Natives: Immigrant bashing on the border* [Motion picture]. United States: Filmaker's Library.

Lightbown, P. & Spada, N. (1999). *How languages are learned.* (2nd ed.) Oxford: Oxford University Press.

Lindlof, T. R., & Taylor, B. C. (2002). *Qualitative communication research methods.* (2nd ed.). Thousand Oaks, CA: Sage.

Maciel, D.R. & Racho, S. (2000). "Yo soy chicano:" The turbulent and heroic life of Chicanas/os in cinema and television. In D. R. Maciel, I. D. Ortiz, and M. Herrera- Sobek (Eds.), *Chicano renaissance: Contemporary cultural trends* (pp. 93-130). Tucson: The University of Arizona Press.

Magaña, L. (2003). *Straddling the border: Immigration policy and the INS.* Austin: University of Texas Press.

Marin, C. (Writer/Director), & MacGregor-Scott, P. (Producer). (1998). *Born in East L.A.* [Motion picture]. United States: Universal.

Marosi, R. (2004, October 23). Decade later, Prop. 187 has an echo in Arizona. *Los Angeles Times*, pp. A1, A12, A13.

Matthews, P. H. (1997). *Oxford concise dictionary of linguistics.* Oxford and New York: Oxford University Press.

McGuire, W. C. (n.d.) *Immigrants and cultural assimilation now.* Retrieved September 1, 2004 from http://www.donovanfitzgerald.com/articles/20020917-1564.shtml

Michelson, M. R. (2001). The effect of national mood on Mexican American political opinion. *Hispanic Journal of Behavioral Sciences, 23*(1), 57-70.

Mitchell, R., & Myles, F. (1998). *Second language learning theories.* London: Arnold. Nava, G. (Director) & Thomas, A. (Producer). (1983). *El norte* [Motion picture]. United States. American Playhouse.

Nevins, J. (2002). *Operation gatekeeper: The rise of the "illegal alien" and the making of the U.S.-Mexico boundary.* New York and London: Routledge.

Nhât Hanh, T. (2003). *Creating true peace: Ending violence in yourself, your family, your community, and the world.* New York: Free Press.

Nichols, B. (1991). *Representing reality: Issues and concepts in documentary.* Bloomington: Indiana University Press.

Noriega, C. A. (2000). *Shot in America.* Minneapolis: University of Minnesota Press. Olendzki, A. (2003). Buddhist psychology. In R. S. Segall (Ed.), *Encountering Buddhism: Western psychology and Buddhist teachings* (pp. 9-30). Albany: State University of New York Press.

Ollman, B. (2002, October). *Why so many exams? A Marxist response.* Retrieved September 11, 2003 from http://www.pipeline.com/~rgibson/whyexams.html

Ono, K. A. & Sloop, J. M. (2002). *Shifting borders: Rhetoric, immigration, and California's proposition 187.* Philadelphia: Temple University Press.

Palafox, J. (2000). *Arizona border: Immigration tensions bring out the worst and the best in human nature.* Retrieved 20 February 2005 from http://www.americaspolicy.org/updater/2000/july07immigrat_body.html#2bookmark2

Perea, J. F. (Ed.). (1997). *Immigrants out!: The new nativism and the anti-immigrant impulse in the United States.* New York and London: New York University Press.

Ponech, T. (1997). What is non-fiction cinema? In R. Allen & M. Smith (Eds.), *Film theory and philosophy* (pp. 203-220). Oxford: Clarendon Press.

Potter, J. (2003). Discourse analysis and discursive psychology. In P. M. Camic, J. E. Rhodes, & L. Yardley (Eds.), *Qualitative research in psychology: Expanding perspectives in methodology and design* (pp. 113-129). Washington, D.C.: American Psychological Association.

Rabiger, J. (1987). *Directing the documentary.* Boston: Focal Press.

Ramirez, A. (1988). Racism toward Hispanics: The culturally monolithic society. In P. A. Katz and D. A. Taylor (Eds.), *Eliminating racism: Profiles in controversy* (pp. 137- 157). New York and London: Plenum Press.

Ratcliff, D. (2003). Video methods in qualitative research. In P. M. Camic, J. E. Rhodes, & L. Yardley (Eds.), *Qualitative research in psychology: Expanding perspectives in methodology and design* (pp. 113-129). Washington, D.C.: American Psychological Association.

Riggins, S. H. (1997). The rhetoric of Othering. In S. H. Riggins (Ed.), *The language and politics of exclusion: Others in discourse* (pp. 1-30). Thousand Oaks, CA: Sage Publications.

Riker, D. (Writer/Director/Editor). (1999). *La ciudad=The city* [Motion picture]. United States: North Star Films.

Rodríguez, N. P. (1997). Social construction of the U.S.-Mexico border. In J. F. Perea (Ed.), *Immigrants out!: The new nativism and the anti-immigrant impulse in the United States.* New York and London: New York University Press.

Ruiz, J. L. (Producer/Director) & Del Olmo, F. (Writer). (1975). *The unwanted* [Motion picture]. United States: National Public Broadcasting Service.

Santa Ana, O. (2002). *Brown tide rising: Metaphors of Latinos in contemporary American public discourse.* Austin: University of Texas Press.

Sayles, J. (Writer/Director). (1996). *Lone star* [Motion picture]. United States: Castle Rock Entertainment.

Shaver, K. G. (1985). *The attribution of blame: Causality, responsibility, and blameworthiness.* New York: Springer-Verlag.

Short, R. & Magaña, L. (2002). Political rhetoric, immigration attitudes, and contemporary prejudice: A Mexican American dilemma. *The Journal of Social Psychology, 142*(6), 701-712.

Simón, L. A. (Director). (1997). *Fear and learning at Hoover Elementary* [Motion picture]. United States: Josepha Producciones.

Smith, R. H., Webster, J. M., Parrott, W. G., & Eyre, H. L. (2002). The role of public exposure in moral and nonmoral shame and guilt. *Journal of Personality and Social Psychology, 83*(1), 138-159.

Snow, M. A. & Brinton, D. M. (Eds.). (1997). *The Content-based classroom: Perspectives on integrating language and content.* White Plains, NY: Longman.

Spencer, G. (Writer/Producer/Editor). (2001). *Conquest of Aztlán: The Mexican takeover of the southwestern U.S.* [Motion picture]. United States: American Patrol / Voices of Citizens Together.

Stam, R. (1989). *Subversive pleasures: Bakhtin, cultural criticism, and film*. Baltimore: The Johns Hopkins University Press.

Stangor, C., & Crandall, C. S. (2000). Threat and the social construction of stigma. In T. F. Heatherton, R. E. Kleck, M. R. Hebl, & J. G. Hebl (Eds.), *The social psychology of stigma* (pp. 62-87). New York and London: The Guilford Press.

Stoller, F. L. & Grabe, W. (1997). A six T's approach to content-based instruction. In M. A. Snow & D. M. Brinton (Eds.), *The content-based classroom: Perspectives on integrating language and content* (pp. 78-94). White Plains, NY: Longman.

Tatalovich, R. (1997). Official English as nativist backlash. In J. F. Perea (Ed.), *Immigrants Out!: The new nativism and the anti-immigrant impulse in the United States* (pp. 78- 102). New York and London: New York University Press.

Tennen, H., & Affleck, G. (1990). Blaming others for threatening events. *Psychological Bulletin, 108*(2), 209-232.

Thurman, R. A. F. (2005). *Anger: The seven deadly sins*. Oxford: Oxford University Press. van den Berg, H., Wetherell, M., & Houtkoop-Steenstra, H. (Eds.). (2003). *Analyzing race talk: Multidisciplinary perspectives on the research interview*. Cambridge: Cambridge University Press.

van Dijk, T. A. (1997). Political discourse and racism: Describing Others in western parliaments. In S. H. Riggins (Ed.), *The language and politics of exclusion: Others in discourse* (pp. 31 – 64). Thousand Oaks, CA: Sage.

van Dijk, T.A. (2001). Principles of critical discourse analysis. In M. Wetherell, S. Taylor, & S. J. Yates (Eds.), *Discourse theory and practice: A reader* (pp. 300-317). London and Thousand Oaks, CA: Sage.

Velasco, J. (2002). Performing multiple identities: Guillermo Gomez-Peña and his "Dangerous Border Crossings." In M. Habell-Pallán & M. Romero (Eds.), *Latino/ a popular culture* (pp. 208-221). New York: New York University Press.

Verkuyten, M. (2003). Racism, happiness, and ideology. In H. van den Berg, M. Wetherell, & H. Houtkoop-Steenstra (Eds.), *Analyzing race talk: Multidisciplinary perspectives on the research intereview* (pp. 138-155). Cambridge: Cambridge University Press.

Welles, O. (Director/Writer). (1958). *Touch of evil* [Motion picture]. United States: Universal.

Wetherell, M. & Potter, J. (1992). *Mapping the language of racism: Discourse and the legitimation of exploitation.* New York: Columbia University Press.

Williams, M. E. (Ed.). (2004). *Immigration: Opposing viewpoints.* Farmington Hills, MI: Greenhaven Press.

Wodak, R. (2001). The discourse-historical approach. In R. Wodak & M. Meyer (Eds.), *Methods of critical discourse analysis,* (pp. 63-94). London: Sage.

www.ingramcontent.com/pod-product-compliance
Lightning Source LLC
Chambersburg PA
CBHW072248310526

45795CB00011B/353